from OUR MOTHERS' KITCHENS

ANITA STEWART

from OUR MOTHERS' KITCHENS

ANITA STEWART

Random House
Toronto

....

Canadian Cataloguing in Publication Data
Stewart, Anita
From our mothers' kitchens
Includes index.
ISBN 0-394-22128-1
1. Cookery, Canadian.   2. Cookery.   I. Title.
TX715.6.S74 1991   641.5971   C90-095920-7

....

DESIGN: Brant Cowie/ArtPlus Limited
COVER PHOTOGRAPH: Hal Roth
FOOD STYLIST: Olga Truchan
PAGE MAKE UP: Dale Bateman/ArtPlus Limited
TYPE OUTPUT: Typeline Express Limited

Printed and bound in Canada

∞

Printed on paper
containing over 50%
recycled paper including
5% post-consumer fibre.

To Mom, with all my love!

ACKNOWLEDGMENTS

•••••••••••••••••••••••••••••••••

T hank you's to all the other special mothers in my life . . . Claire Stewart and the late Meadie Stewart, Glenna Dungey, Kay Fettes, Joan Sarvis, Lynda McGowan, Aletha McArthur and Angela Stewart.

Hugs to my great friends, who coincidentally are also Moms in their own right . . . Eleanor, Lynne, Joan, Vera, Jo-Marie, Lillian and her mom, Lillian, Wyonna and her daughters, Lea Anne and Nancy.

To Peggy Morris and Elaine Mayne, without whom we wouldn't have godparents for our boys.

And many thanks to Barb Nymark, Lillian Kaplun, Pearl Geneen and her great kid, Lucy Waverman, Nancy Turner, Rosemary Brydon, Minnie Fiddler, Linda Myres, Sandra Hall, Frederique Philip, Lena Nafziger, Beatrice Feick and May Thom.

And I mustn't forget to say "I love you!" to my boys . . . Paul, Mark, Brad and Jeff. Without them there would have been no reason to even consider compiling these recipes.

This book is for you all . . . ENJOY IT!

INTRODUCTION

••••••••••••••••••••••••

I love upscale food . . . arugula in my edible flower salad and sea
urchin roe in my soup. But in the dead of winter, or when I'm in
the need of spiritual sustenance, I get out my old red three-ring binder
and sort through all the recipes that have been handed down to me
from my mother, my grandmother, my special friends and their
mothers. Then I spend a few hours in the kitchen — baking bread,
making soup, whipping up my boys' favorite desserts or perhaps even
putting up a batch of jelly.

There are food trends that pass and I am as aware of them as any
food writer. They are fun and exciting, but in their wake, our foodways
are only minimally changed. They leave a few marked benefits — the
lightness of yogurt, the fibre of granola — but we always return to the
dishes we grew up and were nurtured on. Nowhere is the connection
between love and food more evident than in our mothers' kitchens.

My home is south-central Ontario. I have roots that go back five
generations in Wellington and Grey counties. We were farmers right
up until the Second World War when my grandparents moved "into
town" to open a restaurant on Main Street, Mount Forest. When I was
a child, my parents had a small market garden just north of Toronto.
Our cooking and that of the generations that preceded me, reflected
the need to preserve what we grew and then use it up over the
wintertime. In my grandparents' day there was the tradition of the beef
ring where farmers, without the luxury of refrigeration, slaughtered a
steer, butchered it and divided it up amongst those neighbours who
attended. The meat was salted, smoked, canned or used fresh.

There were "bees" when the women would get together to put
down preserves, dry apples and make maple syrup. The threshing
dinners were gargantuan. Sausages, roasts, breads, pickles, vegetables,

cakes and at least half a dozen pies were prepared twice each work day to be piled onto oil-cloth covered trestled tables in the kitchen. Barn raisings were the same. (I still have some of the china that my grandmother used for those dinners.)

When the 1950's came along with Kraft Dinner and other convenience foods, the women in my family thought it was terrific — for a while. But eventually, they all returned to the basics. Although they purchased their meats at the butcher store or even in a supermarket and took part in "progressive suppers," their kitchens again turned out high loaves of golden bread and sweet rolls, warm wintertime dishes such as shepherd's pie with a fluffy mashed potato topping, chicken stew with puffs of dumplings floating all over the surface and fragrant baked beans. With each passing summer and autumn the kitchen wall paper was lifted a little more by all the steam rising off the boiling jams, jellies, preserves and pickles.

But these are the comfort foods of only my little space in Canada. There are creamy buttermilk pies and nutty oatcakes from the Maritimes; cheese-stuffed perogies and juicy Saskatoon berry pie from the Prairies; and spicy cretons and hearty tourtière, tarte au sucre and golden beignets which all spell old-fashioned French Canadian cooking. Our Canadian culinary heritage has been forever enriched because of two centuries worth of immigration. The dishes of the First Peoples, French, English, Irish, Scots, Italian, Mennonite, German and all the other founding peoples of Canada are the foods to which succeeding generations will return.

But this is a cookbook not a historical treatise. The recipes come from scattered regions across Canada. I have talked to individuals, some older members of each community and used their reminiscences in the introduction to their recipes. You will be able to glimpse inside some of the kitchens of Canada . . . not the way we wish they could be, but the way they are.

A KETTLE OF SOUPS

WATERLOO COUNTY BEAN SOUP
WITH HAM AND SMOKED SAUSAGE

The foods of Canada are very regional. It is a sad fact that we, as Canadians, rarely look inwards to appreciate the amazing quality of our foodstuffs. The strength of our culture is in its diversity. Perhaps it's because of our vast distances that communities are still attached to the roots of generations past, yet we can also consider ourselves rampant, died-in-the-wool nationalists. Not too many countries share this privilege.

Last week, we drove out through the snow-covered fields of Waterloo County to purchase some freshly dried beans from a local farmer. They are wonderful — hard, white pearls. As I write, the bean soup that is cooling on the back deck is thick and meaty and as good as any that has ever come from my kitchen. Its smoky flavor comes from the remains of a home-cured ham that I obtained from another farmer, this time in Wellington County. For dessert, the freezer provided some local, organically grown strawberries, which I only have to sweeten with a drizzle of honey, again from a bee-keeper near Arthur. What could be more regional . . . or more Canadian?

1 lb	white beans, thoroughly washed	500 g
12 cups	cold water	3 L
1	large meaty ham bone	1
	OR	
½ lb	unsliced bacon	250 g
½ tsp	salt	2 mL
2 cups	diced celery	500 mL
1 cup	minced onion	250 mL
1	garlic clove, minced	1
1½ cups	diced lean ham	375 mL
½ tsp	pepper	2 mL
1 tsp	dried marjoram	5 mL
¼ cup	minced fresh parsley	50 mL
	OR	
2 tbsp	dried parsley	25 mL
1 lb	smoked sausage, cut into small chunks	500 g

In large soup kettle, cover beans with cold water and let stand for 8 to 10 hours. (If your beans are fresh, reduce standing time to 3 to 4 hours.)

Add ham bone and salt. Cover and bring to a boil. Reduce heat and simmer for 2 hours.

Stir in celery, onion, garlic, ham, pepper and marjoram. Simmer for 1 hour.

Add parsley and smoked sausage. Simmer for 30 minutes.

Makes 10 to 12 servings.

HOMEMADE BEEF STOCK

M aking your own stock is very rewarding . . . it ought to be because it is NOT cheap. Use in any soup recipe — try Beef with Barley (p. 5) — or invent your own.

The amounts are approximate because it's rare that one ever has the exact amounts of all the ingredients.

8 to 10 lb	beef soup bones, some with meat	3.5 to 4.5 kg
1	small can (5 ½ oz /156 mL) tomato paste	1
1	whole garlic bud	1
1 to 2 tsp	whole peppercorns	5 to 10 mL
	Water	
2 or 3	whole cooking onions, unpeeled, chopped	2 or 3
3 or 4	carrots, chopped	3 or 4
2 or 3	celery stalks and leaves, chopped	2 or 3
1 to 2 tsp	dried thyme	5 to 10 mL
2 or 3	bay leaves	2 or 3
1 to 2 tsp	juniper berries* (optional but recommended)	5 to 10 mL
1 to 2 tsp	dried basil	5 to 10 mL

Preheat oven to 400°F (200°C)

Place bones on large, flat baking sheet with sides. Spread bones with tomato paste. Break garlic bud apart and spread around bones along with peppercorns. Roast for 40 to 60 minutes or until bones are very, very dark and tomato paste is deep, rich brown.

Transfer everything to large stock pot. Add enough water to barely cover bones. Toss in onions, carrots, celery, thyme, bay leaves, juniper berries (if using) and basil. Bring to boil, cover and reduce heat. Simmer for 6 hours or until vegetables have lost their color and are very soft.

Remove from heat and strain into large bowl. Skim off fat. Taste and if still a little weak in flavor, return to pot and cook for approximately 1 hour, uncovered, to concentrate it. *Makes 12 to 16 cups (3 to 4 L).*

* These small, dusky blue berries can be picked from any unsprayed juniper tree in late summer through to late fall. You can also purchase them at gourmet specialty shops, but you'll realize that it's more economical to plant a tree!

BEEF WITH BARLEY SOUP

This is a quintessential comfort food . . . rich, meaty and guaranteed to cure the winter blahs. Serve it with homemade bread, perhaps Whole Wheat Buttermilk Soda Bread (p. 136).

The quantities here are approximate. Remember that soup making is a creative exercise and more or less of one ingredient will add the cook's own signature to the soup pot.

4 to 6 cups	Homemade Beef Stock (recipe page 4)	1 to 1.5 L
1	large onion, minced	1
½ cup	pearl barley	125 mL
¾ cup	cubed uncooked beef (stewing beef is fine)	175 mL
2 or 3	carrots, peeled and diced	2 or 3
1 or 2	potatoes, peeled and diced	1 or 2
1 or 2	celery stalks and leaves, diced	1 or 2
½ tsp	dried rosemary (optional) Salt and pepper	2 mL

In heavy soup pot, combine stock, onion, barley and beef cubes. Cover and bring to boil. Reduce heat and simmer for 1½ hours or until barley is swollen and tender.

About 30 minutes before serving, add carrots, potatoes, celery and rosemary. Season to taste with salt and pepper. Simmer until vegetables are cooked but not too soft. *Makes 4 generous servings.*

GRANDMA GENEEN'S CHICKEN SOUP

L ucy Waverman, Sophie Geneen's granddaughter, cooking school teacher, author and food columnist, writes: "It sooths the nerves, cures colds, lowers fevers. This magic drug has unheard-of medical benefits and an aura of mysticism surrounds it. Years of tradition go into its making and its ancestry is very important. It's chicken soup, affectionately known as Jewish penicillin."

Finding the best chicken is a good way to make the best soup. Good chickens are plump, yellow-skinned and fresh. Use full-flavored capons or pullets, older hens often specially fattened to make a rich, full broth.

It is important to cook the soup gently because too high a simmer will cause the broth to go cloudy.

Don't salt until after the soup is cooked. Strain and chill. It is best made the day before to allow the fat to congeal on top for easy removal. Use wherever chicken stock is called for in a recipe or make the richest, most delicious Chicken Noodle Soup with Vegetables (p. 7) you've ever tasted.

1	large (5 lb/2.25 kg) capon, cut into 8 pieces	1
10 cups	cold water	2.5 L
2	onions, cut into chunks	2
3	carrots, cut into chunks	3
3	celery stalks, cut into chunks	3
4	sprigs fresh parsley	4
1	bay leaf	1
1	garlic clove	1

In large soup kettle, cover chicken with cold water and bring to boil over medium heat. Reduce heat and skim thoroughly. Add onions, carrots, celery, parsley, bay leaf and garlic. Simmer, covered, for 4 to 6 hours or until soup is full of flavor. Remove chicken pieces and reserve meat. Strain liquid, chill and remove fat.

Refrigerate or freeze if not using immediately. *Makes about 6 servings.*

CHICKEN NOODLE
SOUP WITH VEGETABLES

Use top-quality egg noodles or make your own by omitting the herbs from Herbed Egg Pasta (p. 45). Beans, peas, celery root, turnip, potato, rice or barley can all be added to provide an infinite number of variations.

To 6 cups (1.5 L) Grandma Geneen's Chicken Soup, add 1 to 2 cups (250 to 500 mL) uncooked noodles; 1 to 2 diced raw carrots; some minced onion; 1 finely chopped celery stalk and some of the reserved chicken meat. Simmer only until vegetables are cooked. Season with salt, pepper and some parsley. *Makes 6 hearty servings.*

SCOTCH BROTH

Homemade Scotch Broth ranks up there with the comfort foods of the world.

2 lb	lamb or mutton shanks (the leaner the better)	1 kg
8 cups	cold water	2 L
2	onions, minced	2
⅔ cup	dried soup vegetables	150 mL
1½ tsp	salt	7 mL
½ tsp	freshly ground pepper	2 mL
2 or 3	diced carrots	2 or 3
1½ cups	diced turnip	375 mL
2 cups	shredded cabbage (optional)	500 mL

In large soup kettle, combine lamb shanks and water. Cover and bring to boil. Add onions, dried soup vegetables, salt and pepper. Reduce heat and simmer gently for 1½ to 2 hours or until meat is very tender.

Remove meat and bones and set aside until cool enough to handle. Skim fat from soup. Add carrots, turnip and cabbage (if using).

Take meat from bones and dice. Return meat to pot. Cook for 30 to 40 minutes or until vegetables are very tender. Serve piping hot.

Makes 6 to 8 servings.

AUNT MAY'S POTATO SOUP

My Aunt May wouldn't tell me that she made this delicious soup from potatoes. In fact, she camouflaged it by adding green food coloring. As an elderly Irish woman, she felt potato soup was a food of the poor. But even after she stopped making it green, I simply loved it.

6 cups	cubed peeled potatoes	1.5 L
1 cup	chopped onions	250 mL
4 cups	chicken or vegetable stock or water	1 L
2 cups	milk	500 mL
	Salt and pepper	
¼ cup	butter, softened	50 mL
2 tbsp	all-purpose flour	25 mL

In large soup kettle or Dutch oven, combine potatoes, onions and stock or water. Cover and bring to boil. Reduce heat and simmer until vegetables are soft, about 20 minutes.

Remove from heat and add milk. Mash with potato masher, or for smooth soup, purée in blender. Return to heat and bring to gentle boil. Season to taste with salt and pepper.

Cream together butter and flour; whisk into soup, stirring constantly until thickened slightly. *Makes 4 to 6 servings.*

VARIATION:

CREAMY MARITIME CHOWDER

Use 3 cups (750 mL) stock (fish or chicken), 1 cup (250 mL) table cream (18%) and 2 cups (500 mL) homogenized milk for the liquids in Aunt May's Potato Soup. Partially cook the vegetables in stock for 20 minutes. Add 1 to 1½ lb (500 to 750 g) cubed uncooked fish, such as cod or halibut. Toss in some scallops or shrimp if you wish . . . perhaps a tin of clams with their juices, or some steamed mussels either whole or shucked. Simmer for 5 minutes longer. Add the milk and cream. Season to taste with salt and pepper. Thicken with the butter/flour mixture. Chowder should be chunky so you don't need to purée it. Toss in some minced fresh parsley to give it a little color. Serve with Crispy Dinner Scones (p. 132). *Makes 6 generous servings.*

FRESH CORN CHOWDER

This is one of my favorite autumn soups. Crisp bacon or sausage may be added before serving, otherwise it's a vegetarian treat.

¼ cup	butter	50 mL
2	large onions, minced	2
1	large sweet green pepper, seeded and diced	1
4 cups	fresh or frozen corn, thawed (about 8 cobs)	1 L
2	large potatoes, peeled and cubed	2
¼ cup	minced fresh parsley	50 mL
¼ cup	all-purpose flour	50 mL
4 cups	milk	1 L
2 cups	heavy cream (35%)	500 mL
	Salt, pepper and Tabasco sauce	

In large soup pot, melt butter. Cook onions and green pepper over low heat for 7 to 10 minutes or until soft. Add corn and continue to cook for 4 to 5 minutes. Stir in potatoes and parsley; cook for 3 minutes.

Whisk flour with a little of the milk; stir into soup until thickened slightly.

Add remaining milk and cream; bring to boil. Cover and reduce heat; simmer for 45 minutes, stirring often. Season to taste with salt, pepper and Tabasco. Serve immediately. *Makes 6 to 8 servings.*

SYLVIA'S MINESTRONE

For a taste of Italy, try this quick soup. The recipe was given to me by Sylvia, a beautiful Roman lady who oversees the Italian pension office in Guelph, Ontario. Top the soup with grated Parmesan and serve it with a basket of crusty rolls.

Sylvia says that you simply clean out your refrigerator for this thick and fragrant soup. Once you've made it, you'll understand that it's incredibly versatile.

¼ cup	unsalted butter	50 mL
1 or 2	large onions, minced	1 or 2
1	garlic clove	1
4 or 6	potatoes, peeled and diced	4 or 6
4 or 6	carrots, peeled and diced	4 or 6
2 or 3	celery stalks, chopped	2 or 3
6 cups	chicken or beef stock or cold water	1.5 L
2 cups	plum tomatoes, peeled and chopped	500 mL
	Salt	
½ tsp	pepper	2 mL
1	large sprig fresh basil (optional)	1
1 cup	each green beans and peas	250 mL
1	can (19 oz/540 mL) Romano beans, drained	1
1 cup	pasta shells or macaroni	250 mL
1 to 2 tbsp	fresh Italian parsley, minced	15 to 25 mL
	Freshly grated Parmesan or Romano cheese	

In heavy soup kettle, melt butter. Add onions and garlic; cook over medium heat until limp and beginning to turn golden. Remove garlic. Add potatoes, carrots and celery; toss to coat with butter and cook for 3 to 4 minutes.

Add stock, tomatoes, salt to taste, pepper, and basil (if using). Cover and simmer for 30 minutes or until vegetables are tender. Add green beans, peas, Romano beans, pasta and parsley. Cook until pasta is tender, 15 to 20 minutes. Remove basil sprig. Pass cheese to sprinkle on each serving. *Makes 8 servings.*

CREAM OF ASPARAGUS
AND WILD LEEK SOUP

To me, the sight of slender spears of asparagus poking up tentatively from the earth is one of the sure signs of spring.

About the same time, tiny wild leeks grow in profusion all over our forests. To harvest them, one must dig them out carefully, shaking off any excess soil. Wash them well and dice the entire plant. Regular cooking onions or cultivated leeks may be substituted if you don't have access to the wild variety. Garnish each bowl with a little chopped dill or a dollop of sour cream.

1 lb	fresh asparagus, cleaned and trimmed	500 g
⅓ cup	butter	75 mL
1 to 1½ cups	finely chopped leeks	250 to 375 mL
5 cups	chicken or vegetable stock	1.25 L
1 tbsp	fresh dill or dried dillweed	15 mL
½ cup	heavy cream (35%)	125 mL
	Salt and pepper	

Cut asparagus into 1-inch (2.5 cm) chunks. Set aside. In heavy saucepan, melt butter over medium-high heat; sauté leeks until tender, 4 to 5 minutes. Add stock and bring to boil. Add asparagus and dill. Reduce heat, cover and simmer until asparagus is tender, about 15 minutes.

Stir in cream. Purée soup in blender or food processor until smooth. Return to saucepan and heat through. Season to taste with salt and pepper. *Makes 4 to 6 servings.*

SOUPE AUX GOURGANES

There is a special bean that is grown in the Charlevoix, Lac St. Jean and Saguenay regions of Quebec. Some beans are saved every year for next year's seed. Although fava beans may be substituted, the rosy-streaked, large green *gourgane* is a true regional specialty.

Diane Gagnon's recipe uses soaked and cooked *gourganes*, which she has canned during the summer. Cover ½ cup (125 mL) dried *gourgane* beans with 1½ cups (375 mL) beef stock and refrigerate overnight. Simmer for 1½ hours or until tender. Or try a 19 oz (540 mL) tin of fava or romano beans. Serve the soup with freshly baked brown bread.

¼ cup	minced salt pork	50 mL
6 to 8 cups	cold water or chicken stock	1.5 to 2 L
1	large onion, minced	1
1 cup	pot barley	250 mL
	Salt and pepper	
½ cup	diced carrots	125 mL
½ cup	diced celery plus leaves	125 mL
2 cups	prepared *gourgane* beans	500 mL
1 tbsp	each minced fresh parsley and *herbes salées** (optional)	

In large saucepan, combine pork and water or stock; bring to boil and cook for 10 minutes. Add onion and barley; season with salt and pepper to taste. Reduce heat to low; cover and simmer for 2 hours or until barley is tender.

Add carrots and celery; cook for 15 to 20 minutes or until vegetables are almost tender. Stir in gourganes; cook for 10 minutes. Stir in parsley and *herbes salées* (if using). Ladle into heated soup bowls.

Makes 6 to 8 servings.

Herbes salées may be purchased throughout Quebec. It is an old way of preserving herbs over the winter and usually includes green onions, shallots, parsley, summer savory, celery, carrots, leeks and lots of coarse salt.

HEARTY SPLIT
PEA SOUP WITH SAUSAGE

M ary and Jack Klein are two of the best bakers we have ever had in our little village. The Kleins like to remove the sausage from the soup to eat on bread . . . a filling, wintertime meal.

2	lean pork hocks	2
10 to 12 cups	water	2.5 to 3 L
1	bag (350 g) split peas	1
3 or 4	leeks, well washed and chopped	3 or 4
2 or 3	carrots, peeled and diced	2 or 3
1	bay leaf	1
	Salt and pepper	
2 tsp	prepared chicken stock base (optional)	10 mL
1 lb	mild smoked sausage	500 g

In large soup kettle, combine pork hocks and water; bring to boil. Add split peas, leeks, carrots and bay leaf. Reduce heat, cover and simmer for 2 to 3 hours or until meat is very tender.

Remove hocks and set aside while soup is simmering until cool enough to handle. Remove and chop all lean bits from bones; return meat to soup, discarding skin, fat and bones. Season to taste with salt, lots of pepper, and chicken stock base (if using).

Add smoked sausage, either whole or in chunks; simmer for 1 hour or until sausage is thoroughly cooked. To serve, ladle into large heated bowls, dividing sausage among bowls. *Makes 8 to 10 servings.*

NORWEGIAN
DILLED GREEN PEA SOUP

Peggy Austin-Johanssen skiis on her snowy mountain daily. Like her late father, the inimitable "Jack Rabbit," her energy seems limitless. This is a refreshing, quick soup that harks back to both her Scandinavian roots and her French-Canadian upbringing. Serve with Sourdough Dark Rye Bread (p. 110) and cheese.

3 cups	fresh or frozen green peas	750 mL
4 cups	Grandma Geneen's Chicken Soup (p. 6)	1 L
¼ tsp	salt	1 mL
¼ tsp	dried dillweed (or 1 tsp/5 mL fresh dill)	1 mL
	Hard-cooked egg, sliced	

If using frozen peas, place in strainer and rinse under cold water to remove ice crystals. In saucepan, combine peas, soup, salt and dillweed. Cover and bring to boil. Reduce heat and simmer for 10 minutes.

Transfer in batches to blender or food processor and purée. Return to saucepan and reheat. Ladle into heated soup bowls. Garnish with slices of hard-cooked egg. *Makes 6 servings.*

SUMMERTIME GAZPACHO SOUP

T his is one of those wonderful seasonal soups that is impossible to
duplicate at any other time of the year. Use the freshest produce,
from a local grower if you can. This recipe may be done in the traditional manner by chopping all the vegetables very finely by hand, or it may
be hastened by chopping them in a food processor or blender. Crumble
the bread with the vegetables or by hand.

8	medium tomatoes, peeled and finely chopped	8
1	cucumber, peeled, seeded (if seeds are large) and diced	1
1	small onion, diced	1
1	garlic clove, minced	1
1	whole pimento or other sweet red pepper, seeded and diced	1
Half	sweet green pepper, seeded and diced	Half
1 cup	crusty bread crumbs	250 mL
¼ cup	fresh lemon juice	50 mL
	Salt and pepper	
	Sour cream	
	Parsley sprigs or chives	

In large bowl, combine tomatoes, cucumber, onion, garlic, pimento,
green pepper and bread. Add lemon juice. Season with salt and pepper
to taste. Cover and chill for at least 4 hours to blend flavors.

Serve icy cold in chilled bowls with generous dollops of sour cream.
Top each with sprig of parsley or chives. *Makes 6 servings.*

CHILLED FRESH TOMATO AND
YOGURT SOUP WITH BASIL

Although sun-ripened, juicy tomatoes bring the very best flavor to this summer soup, canned plum tomatoes may be substituted if necessary. Drain them partially before following the recipe directions. Pass extra yogurt to dollop on each serving if desired.

2 cups	coarsely chopped peeled ripe tomatoes	500 mL
1 cup	plain yogurt	250 mL
1 cup	Grandma Geneen's Chicken Soup (p. 6)	250 mL
8 or 10	large basil leaves, minced	8 or 10
½ tsp	pepper	2 mL
1 tsp	granulated sugar (optional)	5 mL
2	green onions, minced	2
	Garlic Croutons (recipe follows)	

In blender or food processor, purée tomatoes. Pass through sieve or food mill into bowl to remove seeds.

Whisk in yogurt, soup, basil and pepper. Taste and add sugar if needed. Cover and chill for 3 to 4 hours before serving.

Ladle into chilled soup bowls. Sprinkle with green onions and Garlic Croutons. *Makes 4 servings.*

GARLIC CROUTONS

3 tbsp	olive oil	50 mL
1	large garlic clove, minced	1
1½ cups	cubed whole wheat or rye bread	375 mL

In nonstick skillet, heat oil over medium-high heat; sauté garlic until tender. Add bread cubes; sauté for 8 to 10 minutes or until brown and crisp. Let cool and store in airtight container. *Makes 1½ cups (375 mL)*

SALADS,
DRESSINGS AND SAUCES

OLD-FASHIONED CREAMY BOILED
SALAD DRESSING CONCENTRATE

This versatile salad dressing concentrate may be used as is, or in place of mayonnaise on sandwiches. Or dilute one part dressing with two parts milk or even sweet pickle juice to toss with tender, mild-flavored greens just harvested from your garden. This was the only dressing that my mother and grandmother kept on hand before the advent of vinaigrettes. Equal parts of light sour cream and the concentrate make one of the very best potato salad dressings ever invented.

6 tbsp	all-purpose flour	90 mL
6 tbsp	granulated sugar	90 mL
2 tbsp	dry mustard	25 mL
2 tsp	salt	10 mL
⅔ cup	white vinegar	150 mL
3	eggs, separated	3
2½ cups	milk	625 mL

In heavy saucepan or top of double boiler, stir together flour, sugar, mustard and salt until no lumps remain. Whisk in vinegar, egg yolks and milk. Cook over medium heat or rapidly boiling water, stirring constantly, until thickened and pudding-like, 8 to 10 minutes on direct heat, 15 to 20 minutes over boiling water.

In bowl, beat egg whites until foamy; whisk in 1 cup (250 mL) of the hot dressing. Return to saucepan and cook over low heat or simmering water, whisking constantly, for 1 to 2 minutes, or 4 to 5 minutes in double boiler, or until mixture begins to steam again. Pour into clean glass jars and refrigerate for up to 10 days.

Makes 3 ½ cups (875 mL).

NANNA'S RED SALAD DRESSING

E veryone in our family knows this dressing. Though it's a little on the sweet side, it is one of my favorites.

⅓ cup	granulated sugar	75 mL
¼ cup	white vinegar	50 mL
2 tbsp	grated onion	25 mL
1 tsp	paprika	5 mL
½ tsp	salt	2 mL
¼ tsp	pepper	1 mL
½ cup	vegetable oil	125 mL

In food processor or 2-cup (500 mL) jar, blend or shake together sugar, vinegar, onion, paprika, salt and pepper. With motor running, gradually add oil or shake until blended. Refrigerate for 2 to 3 hours before using. *Makes 1 cup (250 mL).*

LIGHT AND SPICY
SOUR CREAM SALAD DRESSING

T his has been one of my favorite dressings for a number of years.

2 cups	light sour cream	500 mL
1 cup	light mayonnaise	250 mL
½ tsp	each pepper, dried sage and garlic powder	2 mL
¼ tsp	each dry mustard, dried marjoram and basil	1 mL
⅛ tsp	cayenne	0.5 mL
¼ cup	grated Parmesan cheese	50 mL

In bowl, stir sour cream with mayonnaise. Add pepper, sage, garlic powder, mustard, marjoram, basil and cayenne. Whisk in cheese. Ladle into glass jar and refrigerate for 2 to 3 hours before using. Store for up to 1 week. *Makes 3 cups (750 mL).*

STEWART'S
ALL-PURPOSE VINAIGRETTE
••

The jungle of weeds that often flourish unchecked in our front garden is incredible! Since the summer is "fix dinner quickly and play a lot" time for me, I turn as many of these weeds as possible into salad.

Consulting Dr. Nancy Turner's book *Edible Garden Weeds of Canada* (National Museum of Natural Sciences), it became clear that nature has blessed us with twice as many salad greens as we had planted. The lamb's quarters that stubbornly grow between my studiously placed rows of lettuce are now in the salad, too. Purslane, with its crisp, paddle-shaped leaves, has spread quickly in our cultivated plot and is, according to Dr. Turner, richer in iron than any other leafy vegetable except parsley. Dandelion greens are an old favorite — our lawn is full of them and I refuse to spray. Have you ever tried the tiny arrow-shaped leaves of sheep's sorrel? Its sour, acidic taste is great in small amounts in salad or in some soups such as potato. I know sorrel spreads easily because one of our gardens is full of it. The whole chicory plant can be used: the leaves as greens, the delicate blue flowers as a garnish and the roots as a coffee substitute. My absolute, all-time favorite weed is the humble "he loves me, he loves me not" Oxeye daisy. It flourishes everywhere in Ontario, so last year I threw some seed into a number of sunny spots in the flower garden. The new spring leaves are excellent and the flowers are edible, too. It is the perfect wild salad green. One hardly needs lettuce.

This basic vinaigrette recipe is best to toss with your freshly harvested wild salad.

Although olive oil and balsamic vinegar are my personal favorites for a wild salad, they may be replaced with a good-quality soy or canola oil and red wine or cider vinegar. I purchase the cheapest Dijon that I can find to give this dressing its unmistakable zip. The garlic may be increased or even omitted.

1 cup	olive oil	250 mL
¼ cup	balsamic, red wine, apple cider or white wine vinegar	50 mL

1 tsp	Dijon-type mustard	5 mL
½ tsp	salt	2 mL
½ tsp	freshly ground black pepper	2 mL
1 to 2 tsp	chopped fresh herbs (basil, oregano, dill or parsley)	5 to 10 mL
1	garlic clove, crushed then minced	1

In glass jar or food processor, shake together oil, vinegar, mustard, salt, pepper, herbs and garlic. Refrigerate for a few hours to allow flavor to develop. *Makes 1¼ cups (300 mL).*

COUNTRY-STYLE POTATO SALAD

The very best potato salads are finished not only with mayonnaise but also with sour cream. This is another very basic recipe that may be altered over the summer with fresh herbs and the addition of chilled, cooked vegetables like beans, carrots, shelled or snap peas. Garnish with lots of chopped fresh dill, green onions or other herbs.

3 lb	new potatoes (unpeeled), scrubbed	1.5 kg
1	large Spanish onion, minced	1
	OR	
3 or 4	green onions, minced	3 or 4
1¼ cups	mayonnaise	300 mL
⅔ cup	sour cream	175 mL
2 tbsp	red wine vinegar or sweet pickle juice	25 mL
2 tsp	granulated sugar	10 mL
	Salt and pepper	

In large pot of boiling water, cook potatoes until tender. Drain and let stand until cool enough to handle. Peel and dice. Place in large bowl along with onion.

In separate bowl, whisk together mayonnaise, sour cream, vinegar and sugar. Season to taste with salt and pepper. Add to warm potatoes and toss gently to mix. Cover and refrigerate for 3 to 4 hours or until well-chilled. *Makes 6 to 8 servings.*

OLD-FASHIONED COLESLAW

This recipe is so delicious that you will never need another coleslaw recipe again! It's also the perfect opportunity to experiment with different kinds of cabbage. You can add any other minced raw vegetables that strike your fancy. Try some green beans, red or green peppers, or unpeeled zucchini.

6 cups	shredded green cabbage	1.5 L
2 or 3	carrots, peeled and grated	2 or 3
1 cup	diced celery plus leaves	250 mL
1 or 2	green onions, minced OR	1 or 2
1	cooking or small Spanish onion, minced	1
¾ to 1 cup	mayonnaise	175 to 250 mL
½ to ⅔ cup	sour cream	125 to 150 mL
1 tbsp	granulated sugar	15 mL
1 tbsp	white or red wine vinegar	15 mL
2 tsp	dried dillweed (optional)	10 mL
1 tsp	celery seeds (optional)	5 mL
	Salt and freshly ground pepper	

In large bowl, toss together cabbage, carrots, celery and onions.

In separate bowl, whisk together mayonnaise, sour cream, sugar, vinegar, and dillweed and celery seed (if using). Season to taste with salt and pepper.

Pour over cabbage mixture and toss to coat thoroughly. Cover and refrigerate for about 1 hour to let flavors blend. *Makes 6 to 8 servings.*

BROCCOLI MUSHROOM SALAD

M y favorite cold vegetable salad!

1	bunch broccoli, cut into pieces	1
3 or 4	large carrots, peeled and sliced	3 or 4
1	small head cauliflower, cut into florets	1
1 lb	fresh mushrooms, thinly sliced	500 g
3 or 4	green onions, thinly sliced	3 or 4
Dressing:		
½ cup	granulated sugar	125 mL
⅓ cup	red wine vinegar	75 mL
1 tsp	salt	5 mL
1 tsp	paprika	5 mL
1 to 2 tsp	celery seeds	5 to 10 mL
1 tsp	onion powder	5 mL
	OR	
¼ cup	minced onion	50 mL
1 cup	vegetable oil	250 mL

In steamer or large, covered pot containing small amount of boiling water, steam broccoli, carrots and cauliflower for 3 to 4 minutes or until tender-crisp. Drain and rinse under cold water to stop cooking; drain well and transfer to large bowl. Add mushrooms and green onions.

Dressing: In small bowl, combine sugar, vinegar, salt, paprika, celery seeds and onion powder; whisk in oil. Pour over prepared vegetables. Refrigerate, covered, for 6 to 8 hours, stirring occasionally. Serve chilled. *Makes 6 to 8 servings.*

PEGGY'S
NORWEGIAN CUCUMBER SALAD

No Norwegian smorgasbord would be complete without this salad. Peggy Austin-Johanssen prepares a number of variations. These are my own favorites.

2	large English cucumbers	2
1 tsp	salt	5 mL
¾ cup	white vinegar	175 mL
2 tbsp	chopped fresh dill	25 mL
1 tbsp	granulated sugar	15 mL
¼ tsp	freshly ground pepper	1 mL
	Lettuce leaves	

Slice cucumbers thinly. Place in glass bowl and sprinkle with salt. Weight down with plate and let stand at room temperature for 2 to 3 hours. Drain completely and pat dry with towel. Place in clean glass bowl.

Stir together vinegar, dill, sugar and pepper; pour over cucumbers and gently stir. Cover and chill for 3 hours. Pour off marinade and serve on lettuce leaves. *Makes 4 to 6 servings.*

VARIATIONS:

CREAMY CUCUMBER SALAD WITH RED ONION

Add 1 thinly sliced red onion to finished Cucumber Salad. Stir together ½ cup (125 mL) sour cream or plain yogurt with 1 tbsp (15 mL) lemon juice; pour over cucumber mixture and stir gently to mix.

CREAMY CUCUMBER SALAD WITH DILL AND RADISHES

Mix together ½ cup (125 mL) sour cream, 1 tbsp (15 mL) minced onion, 1 tbsp (15 mL) minced dill pickle and 1 tbsp (15 mL) lemon juice. Taste and adjust seasoning if necessary with granulated sugar and pepper. Pour over finished Cucumber Salad and stir gently to mix. Sprinkle with ½ cup (125 mL) thinly sliced radishes.

HOT SALAD
OF GREENS WITH CRISP BACON

•••

This tangy salad must be prepared immediately before serving. Vary the greens from spinach to young dandelion leaves, kale or endive.

3 to 4	slices bacon, coarsely chopped	3 to 4
2 tbsp	all-purpose flour	25 mL
3 tbsp	granulated sugar	45 mL
½ tsp	dry mustard	2 mL
½ tsp	salt (optional)	2 mL
¼ cup	cider vinegar	50 mL
¾ cup	half-and-half cream (10%)	175 mL
6 to 8 cups	bite-sized pieces of mixed greens	1.5 to 2 L
2	hard-cooked eggs, chopped	2

In heavy skillet, cook bacon over medium heat until crisp. Remove with slotted spoon and set aside.

Blend flour into fat in skillet; cook, stirring, for a few seconds. Reduce heat to low; stir in sugar, mustard and salt (if using). Whisk in vinegar and cream; cook, stirring, for 2 to 3 minutes or until thickened.

Add greens and toss quickly to coat thoroughly. Tip into salad bowl. Sprinkle with bacon bits and chopped eggs. Serve immediately.

Makes 4 to 6 servings.

FRESH PLUM TOMATO SAUCE

In season, plum tomatoes are available at markets across Canada for bargain-basement prices. Thick and fleshy, they are the only tomatoes that should be used when making an Italian-style sauce. Peel and freeze the tomatoes (no cooking needed) for use throughout the winter. Or if you have time, can them yourself.

I try to keep this meatless sauce on hand most of the time. It has 1,001 uses! Try it over pasta or as a basic cooking sauce to pour over meat balls or to simmer them in. Top browned chicken with a cupful and bake covered for an hour or so. Then top with a mild cheese before serving. It's also great as a base for lasagna or stuffed ravioli.

¼ cup	olive oil	50 mL
3 to 4	garlic cloves, crushed	3 to 4
2	large onions, minced	2
1	can (13 oz/369 mL) tomato paste	1
8 to 10 cups	chopped peeled plum tomatoes OR	2 to 2.5 L
2	cans (each 28 oz/796 mL) plum tomatoes, undrained	2
¼ cup	minced fresh basil OR	50 mL
2 tbsp	dried basil	25 mL
1½ tsp	salt	7 mL
¼ tsp to ½ tsp	red pepper flakes	1 to 2 mL
2 tsp	fennel seeds, coarsely crushed	10 mL
	Pepper	
	Granulated sugar	

In large heavy pot, heat oil over medium heat; cook garlic and onions, stirring, until just beginning to turn golden. Add tomato paste; rinse tin with cold water and add to pot.

Stir in tomatoes, basil, half of the salt, red pepper flakes and fennel seeds; season to taste with pepper. Bring to boil; reduce heat and simmer, uncovered, for 1 hour. Taste and add a little sugar if needed to counteract acidity.

Cook, stirring often, for 1 to 1½ hours longer or until thickened. Season to taste with remaining salt. Use immediately or let cool and seal in glass jars; refrigerate for up to 4 weeks. *Makes 6 to 7 cups (1.5 to 1.75 L).*

QUICK AND EASY BARBECUE SAUCE

Generally, we grill foods that take a minimum of fuss — farmer's sausage, ribs and chicken, all of which I precook on top of the stove for a few minutes. Then all that is needed is a quick finish on the barbecue. Fish needs no precooking, but the grill or fish basket must be well oiled.

Serve with potatoes and onions baked in foil on the grill and a salad.

1 ½ cups	corn syrup	375 mL
1 cup	ketchup	250 mL
½ cup	Worcestershire sauce	125 mL
2 tbsp	Dijon mustard	25 mL
2 tsp	ground ginger	10 mL
1 tsp	chili powder	5 mL
½ tsp to 1 tsp	Tabasco sauce	2 to 5 mL
1 tsp	minced fresh rosemary	5 mL
2	cloves garlic, crushed and minced	2
2 tsp	*herbes de Provence** (optional)	10 mL

In glass jar, shake together corn syrup, ketchup, Worcestershire sauce and mustard. Add ginger, chili powder, Tabasco sauce, rosemary, garlic, and *herbes de Provence* (if using). Cover and shake to mix well. Refrigerate for 1 hour to blend flavors.

Makes 1¾ cups (425 mL).

**herbes de Provence* is a mixture of dried thyme, rosemary, bay, basil and savory that is commonly found in the south of France. It's well worth the effort to obtain and become familiar with using it.

HOLLANDAISE SAUCE

Serve this light and delicious sauce over lightly steamed vegetables. It is especially wonderful over asparagus.

½ cup	unsalted butter	125 mL
3	egg yolks	3
4 tsp	fresh lemon juice	20 mL
2 tsp	water	10 mL
¼ tsp	salt	1 mL
¼ tsp	white pepper	1 mL
1 tsp	Dijon mustard	5 mL
	OR	
½ tsp	dry mustard	2 mL

In small saucepan, melt butter until bubbling but not browned.

Meanwhile, in blender or food processor, combine egg yolks, lemon juice, water, salt, pepper and mustard; blend at low speed for 5 to 10 seconds. With machine still running, pour in half of the hot butter in thin steady stream. Increase speed to high; gradually pour in remaining butter. Serve immediately. *Makes 1 cup (250 mL).*

GARLICKY CLAM SAUCE FOR PASTA

The secret to this great sauce is lots of clams. Serve it over Herbed Egg Pasta (p. 45) or one of the good fresh varieties that are readily available. Serve over hot pasta, and pass around dried hot pepper flakes and lots of grated Parmesan cheese.

¼ cup	olive oil	50 mL
2	garlic cloves, minced	2
1 cup	minced celery	250 mL
1	medium-sized sweet green pepper, seeded and minced	1
1	medium onion, minced	1
2	tins (5 oz/142 g) baby clams, drained and chopped	2
2 to 3 cups	Fresh Plum Tomato Sauce (p. 28) or high-quality purchased sauce	500 to 750 mL

In heavy saucepan, heat oil over medium heat; cook garlic for 1 to 2 minutes or until almost tender. Add celery, green pepper and onion; cook, stirring, until tender, about 10 minutes.

Stir in clams and tomato sauce; bring to boil. Reduce heat and simmer for 2 to 3 minutes only. *Makes 3 to 4 cups (750 mL to 1 L).*

VEGETABLES
AND SUPPER DISHES

SPRING ASPARAGUS
TART WITH CHEESE
....

All that is needed with this taste of spring is a green salad tossed
with Light and Spicy Sour Cream Salad Dressing (p. 20), and
perhaps some crusty rolls. The choice of cheeses is up to you. You can
substitute chèvre, a mild and creamy goat's milk cheese, for the cream
cheese, and Gaisli, an aged goat's milk cheese, for the Monterey Jack.

½ lb	fresh asparagus	250 g
	One 10″ (25 cm) unbaked pie shell	
½ lb	cream cheese, softened	250 g
½ lb	Monterey Jack, Havarti	250 g
	or Oka cheese, grated or	
	finely chopped	
½ cup	milk	125 mL
4	eggs	4
1 tbsp	cornstarch	15 mL
1 tbsp	lemon juice	15 mL
¼ tsp	salt	1 mL
¼ tsp	pepper	1 mL
2 tbsp	minced fresh chives	25 mL
1 tsp	minced fresh thyme (optional)	5 mL

Preheat oven to 400°F (200°C).

In saucepan of small amount of boiling water, cook asparagus until
barely tender. Drain and arrange in pie shell.

In large bowl, beat together cream cheese and Monterey Jack. Beat
in milk, eggs, cornstarch, lemon juice, salt, pepper, chives and thyme
(if using). Pour over asparagus. Bake for 35 to 40 minutes or until
centre is set and top is golden. *Makes 8 servings.*

MY MOTHER'S
MACARONI AND CHEESE
•••••••••••••••••••••••••••••••••••••••

S ince I was a little girl, my mother warmed my heart with this creamy, delicious casserole topped with lots of buttered bread crumbs. I still love it — especially with The Chili Sauce Recipe (p. 79) and thick slices of yeasty Herbed Batter Bread (p. 121).

2 cups	elbow macaroni	500 mL
½ cup	butter or bacon drippings	125 mL
3 tbsp	all-purpose flour	50 mL
¾ tsp	salt	4 mL
½ tsp	dry mustard	2 mL
½ tsp	pepper	2 mL
2 cups	hot milk	500 mL
1	medium onion, minced	1
2 cups	shredded medium or old Cheddar cheese	500 mL
1 cup	soft bread crumbs	250 mL

Preheat oven to 400°F (200°C).

In large pot of lightly salted boiling water, cook macaroni until tender but firm. Drain and set aside.

Meanwhile, in heavy saucepan, melt ¼ cup (50 mL) of the butter over medium heat; stir in flour, salt, mustard and pepper. Cook, stirring, for 1 minute, without browning. Whisk in hot milk and onion; cook, stirring, until thickened, about 5 minutes. Add cheese and stir until melted. Combine with cooked macaroni and pour into well-buttered 6-cup (1.5 L) casserole. Set aside.

In skillet, melt remaining butter over medium heat; add bread crumbs and cook, stirring, until golden. Sprinkle evenly over casserole. Bake, uncovered, for 20 minutes or until bubbly and crusty.

Makes 4 generous servings.

CLEAN-OUT-THE-REFRIGERATOR
CRUSTLESS QUICHE

I t may be hard to believe, but there are definitely occasions when I don't have the time or the inclination to cook. That's when my sons pitch in and in their own teenaged, somewhat sloppy way create wonderous, unrecognizable dishes of dubious merit. But at least they've tried and when they leave home they won't be totally helpless in the kitchen. I try to give them easy recipes, adolescent-proof at least to some extent.

If you can convince your crew to pick up a spoon and lend a hand, this recipe is guaranteed to give positive encouragement to even the beginning cook. I've suggested just a few of the potential additions. It all depends on the variety in your fridge! Serve this easy supper dish with a green salad, pickles and a loaf of Herbed Onion Beer Bread (p. 135).

4	eggs	4
1¾ cups	milk	425 mL
¼ cup	melted butter or margarine	50 mL
½ cup	unbleached all-purpose flour	125 mL
¼ tsp	salt	1 mL
½ tsp	baking powder	2 mL
1½ cups	diced cooked ham, cooked sausage, green pepper, green onion, sliced mushrooms or steamed broccoli	375 mL
2 cups	shredded cheese	500 mL

Preheat oven to 350°F (180°C). Grease 9-inch (23 cm) pie plate.

In large mixing bowl, whisk together eggs, milk and butter; set aside. Stir or sift together flour, salt and baking powder; add to egg mixture.

Fold in meats and/or vegetables. Pour into prepared pan. Sprinkle evenly with cheese. Bake for 50 to 60 minutes or until golden and puffed. Let stand for 10 minutes before serving. *Makes 6 servings.*

LYNNE'S MARVELLOUS BAKED BEANS

These are my all-time favorite baked beans . . . very French and very good. Serve with a large green salad and whole wheat bread. Leftovers, if there are any, may be frozen.

4 cups	dried white pea (navy) beans	1 L
12 cups	cold water	3 L
2	garlic cloves	2
2 tsp	dried thyme	10 mL
1	bay leaf	1
⅛ tsp	ground allspice	0.5 mL
1 lb	salt pork, rinsed and thinly sliced	500 g
2	onions, minced	2
1	can (4 oz/114 mL) tomato paste	1
1½ cups	packed brown sugar	375 mL
1 tsp	dry mustard	5 mL
½ cup	butter, softened	125 mL
4	apples, cored and sliced	4
½ cup	dark rum	125 mL
¼ cup	maple syrup	50 mL
¼ cup	fancy molasses	50 mL

Wash beans thoroughly. Cover with cold water and soak overnight. Turn beans and water into large saucepan; add garlic, thyme, bay leaf and allspice. Bring to boil; reduce heat and simmer, covered, for 1 hour.

Preheat oven to 325°F (160°C). Line large roasting pan or bean pot with salt pork.

To bean mixture, add onions, tomato paste, 1 cup (250 mL) of the brown sugar and mustard; stir to blend. Pour into prepared pan; cover and bake for 3 hours, adding water if necessary and stirring occasionally.

Cream butter with remaining sugar; spread over beans. Arrange apples evenly over top; drizzle with rum, maple syrup and molasses. Bake for 1 to 1½ hours longer or until richly browned and tender.

Makes 10 to 12 servings.

MINNIE'S PEROGIES

Although she now lives in Medicine Hat, Alberta, Minnie Fiddler grew up in northern Saskatchewan. Isolated from so-called civilization, her family worked from dawn to dusk. The following is a small page of our national history gleaned from a letter Minnie wrote to me several years ago describing her rural prairie life. When my own mother (fifth generation central Ontarian) read it, she said, "My, that's just how it was for our family too."

******

"We had a small dairy business on the farm and used to supply the town of Garrick with milk, cream and butter. We separated the milk with a hand separator, then Mom would let skim milk sit at room temperature till it was like jelly and hang it to drip. That was our cottage cheese.

"We smoked our own bacon in the smoke house and canned a lot of meatballs. Mom canned pork chunks in quart sealers with spices. We used to have pork roasts boiled with white beans. She rendered her own lard from the fat.

"In the summer, when my uncle went fishing, he always brought us some trout, which we dipped in flour, salt and pepper, then fried. We raised a lot of chickens, turkeys and geese so had a cellar full of canned chicken meat and a goose or turkey for Christmas. The rest we would sell. We also sold eggs.

"We always had a big garden that kept us in vegetables all year. The carrots, peas, beans and corn were canned. Mom bought fruit with the money from the fowl and preserved it. She saved all the down from the geese and I am still using the pillows today. We always made sauerkraut in a 10-gallon crock with a plate weighted down with a stone.

"We had lots of blueberries, which we picked up north in the muskeg, pin cherries and chokecherries. These we made into jams and jellies. We grew our own strawberries, raspberries and lots of saskatoons. We also had a hazelnut tree and a gooseberry bush.

"Mom made her own soap for washing clothes. She made lots of dill, mustard and beet pickles. Our cellar was always full of preserves made with sugar as honey was scarce . . . nobody kept bees.

"We ate a lot of perogies, stuffed with our cottage cheese and cabbage rolls made with ground pork, rice, onions, salt and pepper. She created all her own salad dressings and pancake syrup. The only groceries we had to buy were flour, sugar, salt, spices, tea and coffee.

"In summer, we ate a lot of lettuce salads with homemade dressing and sliced cucumbers with sour cream, salt and pepper. For porridge we ground our own wheat and flax." (April 2, 1989/Medicine Hat, Alberta)

******

This typically Ukranian dish of perogies is one that everyone should taste at least once in a lifetime. Nowadays, we don't have to make our own cottage cheese, but since the traditional dry curd cheese is rarely available, rinse the creamed variety thoroughly under cold running water before letting it drain for 45 to 60 minutes. To serve, pass bowls of sour cream liberally laced with green onion and chopped onion that has been lightly browned in butter and served plain or mixed with a little heavy cream. Sprinkle crumbled crisp bacon on top of perogies.

Although perogies are served as a main course, they make terrific soup dumplings. Simply drop into the boiling broth during the final 15 minutes of cooking.

Dough:

2	eggs	2
1 tsp	salt	5 mL
1 cup	cold water	250 mL
3 cups	all-purpose flour	750 mL

Filling:

6	potatoes, peeled and boiled	6
2	onions, peeled and finely chopped	2
2 tbsp	butter	25 mL
2 cups	cottage cheese, rinsed and drained	500 mL
	Salt and pepper	

Dough: In bowl, beat eggs well. Whisk in salt and water. Beat in flour to make stiff dough. Turn dough out onto floured surface; knead until smooth, 3 to 5 minutes. Cover and refrigerate while preparing filling.

Filling: Mash potatoes well. In small skillet, cook onions in butter until browned; stir into potatoes along with cottage cheese. Season to taste with salt and pepper. Set aside.

Assembly: On lightly floured surface, roll out dough as thinly as possible; cut into 2-inch (5 cm) squares. With floured fingers, pick up a square and stretch slightly; put small spoonful of filling into centre and pinch shut. Lay on floured baking sheet and cover. Repeat with remaining squares and filling.

Bring large pot of salted water to boil. Reduce to medium and cook 6 to 8 perogies at a time until they float to the top, about 10 minutes. Remove with slotted spoon; toss with a little butter and keep warm while cooking remaining perogies. (Perogies can be frozen on covered baking sheet, then packaged in plastic bags. Frozen perogies may be cooked in the same manner as above, but for about 12 minutes.) *Makes about 3 dozen or 6 servings.*

HOLUBCHI
(UKRANIAN CABBAGE ROLLS)

Anne Kuziack, who lives in Yorkton, northeast of Regina, Saskatchewan, explained the differences in cabbage rolls to me. The Ukranian version is meatless. Originally the rolls were made with whole cabbage leaves pickled in brine. Most cooks prefer sweet cabbage now — the large, somewhat flattened heads with leaves that aren't too tightly grown.

Remove the core of the cabbage with a sharp knife and pour boiling water into the cavity. Let it stand for 5 to 6 minutes to soften the leaves. After discarding the hot water, peel the leaves off, place them on to a baking sheet and pop them into the freezer for 30 minutes to soften a little further. When the leaves thaw, they are flexible and easy to work with. When rolling each roll, fold one side inward and then roll the filled leaf into a cone shape. Serve with additional onions which have been sautéed in butter.

Line your buttered or oiled roasting pan with the bits of cabbage remaining after making the rolls.

1	large head green cabbage	1
3 to 4	onions, minced	3 to 4
⅓ cup	butter or vegetable oil	75 mL
3 cups	cooked rice	750 mL
2 to 3 tsp	dried dillweed	10 to 15 mL
1½ tsp	salt	7 mL
¾ tsp	pepper	4 mL
2 cups	tomato sauce	500 mL
	PLUS	
2 tsp	granulated sugar	10 mL
	OR	
1	can (10 oz/284 mL) condensed tomato soup	1
	Butter	

Prepare cabbage leaves as above.

In skillet, sauté onions in butter until just beginning to turn golden.

In bowl, combine rice, onions, dillweed, salt and pepper. Let cool enough to handle.

Preheat oven to 350°F (180°C)

Cut large cabbage leaves in half or thirds and place flat on work surface. Spoon some of the filling onto each piece and roll up, folding in edges. Arrange in layers in prepared roasting pan. Pour on water until you can just see it. Add tomato sauce and sugar or tomato soup diluted with equal amount of water. Dot liberally with butter. Cover tightly and bake for 1½ hours. *Makes 10 to 12 servings.*

BARLEY AND MUSHROOM
CASSEROLE WITH ALMONDS
•••

L illian Kaplun suggests that ½ lb (250 g) of lightly sautéed chicken livers can be stirred into this delicious casserole during the final 15 minutes of baking.

¼ cup	butter or margarine	50 mL
1	large onion, diced	1
½ cup	finely chopped celery	125 mL
¼ cup	finely chopped sweet green or red pepper	50 mL
1 cup	pearl barley	250 mL
2 cups	hot chicken or beef stock	500 mL
½ lb	fresh mushrooms, sliced Salt and pepper	250 g
⅓ cup	slivered almonds	75 mL

Preheat oven to 350°F (180°C).

In large skillet, melt butter over medium heat; cook onion, celery and green or red pepper, stirring, for 1 to 2 minutes or until onion is barely tender. Add barley and cook for 3 to 4 minutes or until beginning to brown. Transfer to buttered, heatproof 8-cup (2L) casserole.

Stir in stock and mushrooms. Season to taste with salt and pepper. Cover and bake for 45 minutes. Sprinkle with almonds; bake, uncovered, for 15 minutes. Serve hot. *Makes 6 to 8 servings.*

FRESH BASIL-WALNUT PASTA

V ary the cheese in this recipe to use up any little leftovers. Or splurge and use freshly grated Romano or Parmesan. Serve with crusty bread, a green salad and perhaps a bottle of dry red Italian wine.

1 lb	fresh Herbed Egg Pasta (p. 45)	500 g
2 tbsp	vegetable oil	25 mL
⅓ cup	butter	75 mL
1	each large sweet red and green pepper, seeded and diced	1
2	shallots or green onions, minced	2
½ cup	minced fresh basil OR	125 mL
¼ cup	dried basil	50 mL
½ cup	chopped walnuts	125 mL
5 or 6	large fresh mushrooms, thinly sliced	5 or 6
½ cup	freshly grated Romano or Parmesan cheese	125 mL

In large pot of boiling lightly salted water, cook pasta until tender but firm. Drain and rinse under hot water; toss with oil to prevent sticking. Keep warm.

Meanwhile, in skillet, melt butter over medium heat; cook red and green peppers, shallots, basil and walnuts, stirring, until peppers are tender-crisp and still brightly colored. Add mushrooms; cook, stirring for 10 to 15 seconds.

In large heated bowl, toss together pasta, vegetable mixture and cheese. Serve immediately. *Makes 4 servings.*

HERBED EGG PASTA

Tiny herb leaves are rolled right into the pasta dough to zip up the flavor. Dry* the pasta or use it fresh.

2 cups	all-purpose flour	500 mL
½ tsp	salt	2 mL
3	eggs	3
1 tbsp	vegetable oil	15 mL
	Fresh herbs (such as parsley, oregano, basil or dill)	
	Pesto (p. 92)	

In bowl, stir together flour and salt. Blend eggs with oil; add all at once to flour. Stir to combine well.

Turn out dough onto floured board. Knead for 5 to 7 minutes or until smooth. Cover with plastic wrap and let stand for 15 minutes.

By hand or in pasta machine, roll out dough until as thin as possible. Scatter fresh herb leaves on half; fold other half over herbs and re-roll until very thin. Cut into desired shapes.

Dry pasta or cook in boiling salted water just until tender but firm, about 4 minutes. Drain and toss with a little vegetable oil to prevent sticking. Serve immediately with Pesto. *Makes 6 servings.*

*To dry pasta. Hang pasta over clean wooden dowels or a broom handle covered with a layer of waxed paper. Suspend your improvised drying rack between two kitchen chairs and let pasta hang until brittle. Store in a tightly covered container.

CRISPY POTATO PANCAKES

This is a wonderful fishing-season emergency dish for the times when that perfect glistening trout doesn't bite. Serve with lots of light sour cream, applesauce, or even maple syrup.

1	large onion, finely grated	1
6	large potatoes, peeled and grated	6
3	eggs, lightly beaten	3
¼ cup	all-purpose flour	50 mL
1 tsp	salt	5 mL
1 tsp	baking powder	5 mL
	Melted butter or oil for frying	

In large bowl, combine onion, potatoes, eggs, flour, salt and baking powder. Lightly butter heavy skillet; heat over medium heat until hot.

Drop about ¼ cup (50 mL) batter for each pancake into hot skillet, pressing down lightly to spread each pancake. Cook for 3 to 5 minutes, flipping pancake over, or until well browned on both sides.

Makes 4 or 5 servings.

CHEESE CLOUD

●●●●●●●●●●●●●●●●●●●●●●●

T his easy supper or brunch dish should be assembled 6 to 12 hours ahead of baking. Pop it into the oven while you enjoy a coffee with your friends . . . then have a great breakfast. Serve hot with sausages or bacon and lots of fresh fruit.

12	slices day-old bread	12
12	slices Cheddar cheese, cut same size as bread	12
6	thin slices ham	6
4	eggs	4
2½ cups	milk	625 mL
½ tsp	Dijon mustard	2 mL
1	small onion, grated	1
¼ tsp	salt	1 mL
⅛ tsp	cayenne pepper	0.5 mL
⅛ tsp	black pepper	0.5 mL
1 tsp	seasoned salt	5 mL

Trim crust from bread; arrange 6 of the slices on bottom of buttered 13- x 9-inch (3 L) baking dish. Cover with cheese and ham. Top with remaining bread.

In bowl, whisk together eggs, milk, mustard, onion, salt, cayenne and black peppers and seasoned salt; pour over bread. Cover and refrigerate for 6 to 12 hours.

Preheat oven to 325°F (160°C).

Bake, uncovered, for 1 hour or until browned and puffed.

Makes 6 servings.

CREAMY SCALLOPED POTATOES

Old potatoes, as opposed to new ones, are the best for this most traditional of recipes. Bake it at the same time you are roasting your ham, meatloaf or whatever. Wrap a well-scrubbed, seeded squash in foil, stuff it into the oven beside the potatoes and dinner will be almost ready.

¼ cup	butter	50 mL
¼ cup	all-purpose flour	50 mL
1 tsp	dry mustard	5 mL
1 tsp	salt	5 mL
½ tsp	pepper	2 mL
2½ to 3 cups	milk	625 to 750 mL
6 cups	sliced peeled potatoes	1.5 L
2 or 3	onions, minced	2 or 3
1 cup	shredded Cheddar cheese	250 mL

Preheat oven to 325°F (160°C) or 350°F (180°C)

In heavy saucepan, melt butter over medium heat; stir in flour and cook, stirring, for 1 minute. Add mustard, salt and pepper; cook for 10 to 15 seconds. Whisk in milk and cook, stirring constantly, until thickened and bubbling.

Pour one-quarter of the sauce into buttered 8-cup (2 L) casserole. Top with layers of potatoes, onions and remaining sauce, ending with sauce on top.

Cover and bake for 1½ hours at 350°F (180°C) or 2 hours at 325°F (160°C) or until potatoes are tender. Sprinkle with cheese and continue to bake until melted. *Makes 6 to 8 servings.*

BABY BEETS AND TOPS TOSSED
WITH FRESH DILL BUTTER

●●

Few summer dishes could be simpler or more delicious.

12	baby beets with greens	12
1 tbsp	minced fresh dill	15 mL
3 tbsp	butter	50 mL

Remove beet greens and wash thoroughly. Drain and set aside. Scrub beets.

In medium-sized saucepan, cover beets with just enough water to barely cover; bring to boil. Reduce heat to medium and cook until tender, about 10 minutes. Drain beets and peel under cold running water; set aside in warm bowl.

Meanwhile, in separate saucepan, combine beet greens with 2 tbsp (25 mL) water; cover tightly and steam until wilted, 5 to 7 minutes. Add to beets along with dill and butter; toss to mix and serve immediately. *Makes 4 to 6 servings.*

MUSHROOMS IN SOUR CREAM
••

This is a great side dish to serve with steak and baked potatoes or as an easy supper dish on toast.

Sauté 1 minced onion in 3 tbsp (50 mL) butter until softened. Add about 1 lb (500 g) sliced mushrooms and cook until excess liquid has evaporated. Season with a little salt, paprika and pepper. Stir into 1 cup (250 mL) sour cream along with ¼ cup (50 mL) chopped fresh parsley.

DUTCH KALE AND MASHED POTATOES
••

Kale simply wasn't part of my own traditional food. But for many Europeans, it was almost a staple. The Dutch folk in our area of Wellington County in Ontario often have the frilly plants gracing their gardens along with a healthy crop of leeks.

Mary Klein explained how they serve it at home. Generally, it's boiled with about twice as much potato. When the vegetables are tender, she simply mashes them together, seasoning them with salt and pepper. Each person sprinkles a little white vinegar over his portion. It is generally served with grilled farm-style sausage.

WINTER TOMATOES
•••••••••••••••••••••••••••••

This was a dish we often ate during the winter when I was young. Serve it hot, in small bowls, with pork chops or sausage.

In small saucepan, combine 3 cups (750 mL) undrained canned tomatoes with 5 slices of shredded white bread and 1 small minced onion. Stir in 1 tbsp (15 mL) granulated sugar. Season to taste with salt and pepper. Heat until beginning to boil. Reduce heat and simmer, covered, for about 10 minutes. Makes 4 to 6 servings.

PASSE PIERRE
•••••••••••••••••••••

Known also as "samphire," "sea beans," "glasswort" or technically as "Salicornia europaea," these slender stalks are picked in the spring and early summer from the salt marshes throughout the Maritimes and in scattered regions of British Columbia to be cooked as a vegetable. Its pleasant salty crunch is lately showing up in "gourmet" dining havens in New York City, but has generally been ignored by the rest of North America.

It is best cooked like you would asparagus, tied in small bundles then steamed or boiled. Leave the woody stalk on while you cook the Passe Pierre, picking the stalks up with your fingers to eat them with melted butter.

MEATS AND FISH — FROM ROAST CHICKEN TO BARBECUED TROUT

FRAGRANT ROAST
CHICKEN WITH PAN GRAVY
••

What is your ultimate comfort food? From Kerry Sear, the former executive chef at Toronto's fabulous Four Season's Hotel, to Anne Desjardins, chef-owner of one of Canada's finest inns, L'eau à la Bouche, to my kids, the answer is the same — roast chicken.

But is there a recipe? Probably not . . . just a method and some cooking times. This is how I prepare a roast chicken.

Take one large 6 to 8 lb (2.5 to 3.5 kg) capon. Wash it and pat it really dry. Rub it all over with either olive oil or melted butter. (I use my hands.) Sprinkle the capon generously with your favorite herb. I use about 2 to 3 tsp (10 to 15 mL) of *herbes de Provence* or crumbled dried marjoram, a sprinkle of salt and some freshly ground pepper. In Quebec and the Atlantic provinces, the favorite herb is summer savory, sold by the bagful in Newfoundland. Place the capon in an uncovered roasting pan and pop into a preheated 350°F (180°C) oven. Roast, basting every now and then, for 30 to 35 minutes per pound (60 to 70 minutes per kilogram) or until meat thermometer registers 185°F (85°C).

When richly golden, remove the chicken from the pan and keep warm. Skim off 3 tbsp (50 mL) fat and discard remaining fat, reserving pan juices. Place the pan over medium heat on the stove top and add the reserved 3 tbsp (50 mL) fat. When hot, add 3 tbsp (50 mL) flour. Cook, stirring, for about 1 minute or until brown and bubbling. Whisk in the pan juices, adding chicken stock if necessary. Cook, stirring, over medium heat until thickened. Pour into a warm gravy boat.

Serve the chicken with whipped mashed potatoes and the gravy, plus whatever else brings back memories of childhood.

Makes 6 to 8 servings.

CHICKEN AND DUMPLINGS

I f you can find a range-fed chicken that's not too young and reasonably meaty, you'll have a wonderful treat.

1	large boiler chicken (3 to 5 lb/1.5 to 2.2 kg)	1
1 tsp	salt	5 mL
2 cups	diced celery and leaves	500 mL
2	medium onions, diced	2
1½ cups	diced carrots	375 mL
1 cup	diced peeled turnip	250 mL
1 cup	fresh or thawed peas	250 mL
1	small tomato, peeled and chopped	1
½ tsp	pepper	2 mL
½ tsp	dried thyme	2 mL
1 or 2	bay leaves	1 or 2
¼ cup	minced fresh parsley	50 mL
Dumplings:		
1 cup	all-purpose flour	250 mL
1 tbsp	baking powder	15 mL
½ tsp	salt	2 mL
¼ cup	chilled butter or shortening	50 mL
⅓ cup	milk	75 mL

In large soup kettle, barely cover chicken with cold water; add salt and bring to boil. Cover, reduce heat and simmer for 2 to 3 hours or until meat is tender. Remove chicken from stock; let cool and remove meat from bones.

Meanwhile, add celery, onions, carrots, turnip, peas and tomato to stock. Season with pepper, thyme, bay leaves and parsley. Simmer, covered, until vegetables are tender. Taste and correct seasonings if necessary. Add chicken meat and stir. Remove bay leaves.

Dumplings: In bowl, stir together flour, baking powder and salt; cut in butter until in fine crumbs. Add milk all at once and stir quickly to blend. Drop batter by spoonfuls onto simmering liquid. Cover tightly and cook over medium heat for 7 minutes or until dumplings are more than double in size. Do not uncover during cooking or steam will escape. *Makes 6 to 8 servings.*

GINGERY MAPLE-GLAZED CHICKEN

I always serve this family favorite with fluffy steamed rice and a large green salad that has half the garden in it. Serve the chicken on a hot platter and garnish with minced green onions or garlic chives, including the blossoms.

2 lb	chicken drumsticks	1 kg
⅓ cup	all-purpose flour	75 mL
¼ cup	vegetable oil	50 mL
½ cup	dark or medium maple syrup	125 mL
2 tbsp	cider vinegar	25 mL
2	large garlic cloves, minced (optional)	2
2 tbsp	soy sauce	25 mL
2 tbsp	dry sherry	25 mL
2 tsp	ginger	10 mL
½ tsp	pepper	2 mL

Preheat oven to 325°F (160°C).

Dredge chicken in flour, shaking off any excess. In nonstick skillet, heat oil over medium heat; brown chicken on all sides until golden. Place drumsticks in single layer in 13- x 9-inch (3.5 L) baking dish.

Whisk together maple syrup, vinegar, garlic (if using), soy sauce, sherry, ginger and pepper; pour over chicken. Bake, uncovered, for 1 hour and 15 minutes or until juices run clear when chicken is pierced, turning chicken every 15 minutes to coat with glaze.

Makes 4 to 6 servings.

PEPPERY BRANDIED PÂTÉ

L iver really isn't on my list of favorite foods, but this pâté is truly delicious. Spiked with lots of crushed black pepper, it is perfect on dark rye bread with a side dish of Mother Mayne's Mustard Pickles (p. 81).

If you have a pot of fresh rosemary, use the chopped leaves in the recipe, then garnish the finished pâté with the whole leaves as well as more crushed black pepper.

½ lb	bacon, diced	250 g
2	medium onions, minced	2
1½ lb	chicken livers, well trimmed	750 g
½ cup	minced celery leaves	125 mL
1½ tsp	dried thyme	7 mL
½ tsp	dried rosemary, crushed	2 mL
½ cup	half-and-half (10%) or table (18%) cream	125 mL
1	bay leaf	1
¼ cup	brandy	50 mL
2 tbsp	crushed black peppercorns	25 mL
½ cup	clarified butter*	125 mL

In heavy covered skillet, cook bacon slowly over low heat until limp and droplets begin to collect. Add onions and cook until onions are softened but not browned. Add chicken livers and cook, stirring, until no longer pink inside, 10 to 15 minutes.

Transfer to food processor and purée, adding celery leaves, thyme, rosemary and cream. Pour into top of double boiler over simmering water. Stir in bay leaf, brandy, peppercorns and ¼ cup (50 mL) of the butter. Cover and cook for 50 to 60 minutes or until mixture thickens and begins to steam. Remove bay leaf. Taste and correct seasoning if necessary.

Transfer to serving bowls or pottery tubs. Pour remaining butter over top to seal. Let cool and refrigerate for up to 1 week.

Makes about 6 cups (1.5 L).

* To clarify butter, place butter in a small saucepan over low heat. When melted, skim off the clear liquid; discard the solids.

TOURTIÈRE DE CHIBOUGAMAU

The tourtière of the Lac St. Jean region is very different from that of other areas in Quebec. It's a hearty, meat-and-potato pie that sticks to the ribs of a people who spend hours in the cold, and I mean cold, outdoors.

This recipe comes from the kitchen of Diane Gagnon and her daughters, Karine, Stephanie and Caroline, who live in the wintry northern town of Chibougamau. Serve hot from the oven with Spicy Pickled Beets (p. 78) and homemade bread.

	Filling:	
2 lb	½ inch (1 cm) cubes of beef and a little salt pork	1 kg
5 lb	potatoes, peeled and cut in ½ inch (1 cm) cubes	2.25 kg
1	large onion, minced	1
1 tsp	salt	5 mL
½ tsp	pepper	2 mL
¾ tsp	dried thyme	4 mL
	Pastry:	
3 cups	all-purpose flour	750 mL
½ tsp	baking powder	2 mL
½ tsp	salt	2 mL
½ lb	cold shortening	250 g
½ cup	(approx) ice water	125 mL

Filling: In large bowl, combine meat, potatoes, onion, salt, pepper and thyme. Cover and refrigerate for 12 hours.

Preheat oven to 450°F (230°C).

Pastry: In large bowl, stir or sift together flour, baking powder and salt; cut in shortening until in fine crumbs. With fork, blend in enough of the ice water until dough can be gathered into ball.

On floured board, roll out two-thirds of the dough into large rectangle; line 20-cup (5 L) casserole or Dutch oven. Pour in filling and spread evenly. Add 2½ to 3 cups (625 to 750 mL) water just until you can just see it through filling. Roll out remaining pastry and cover pie. Trim and crimp edges. Slash steam vents in top.

Bake for 15 minutes. Reduce heat to 325°F (160°C) and bake for 4 hours longer or until tourtière is a rich brown, covering if top becomes too dark. *Makes 12 to 15 servings.*

CHUNKY BEEF STEW

To make this hearty stew into a meat pie, simply pour the stew into a lightly oiled casserole and top with either pie crust or thinly rolled biscuit dough.

The recipe is one that rarely remains the same — add whatever hearty vegetable you'd like to create your own version. You may decide to substitute pork or lamb, or even venison, in which case you might like to add a shot of full-bodied red wine to the cooking liquid. Ladle the stew into hot bowls and serve with homemade bread and a salad. What else could ever be needed?

2 to 3 lb	lean stewing beef, cut into 1-inch (2.5 cm) cubes	1 to 1.5 kg
½ cup	all-purpose flour	125 mL
½ tsp	pepper	2 mL
¼ to ⅓ cup	vegetable oil	50 to 75 mL
3 or 4	onions	3 or 4
2 ½ cups	tomato juice or canned tomatoes	625 mL
2 cups	Homemade Beef Stock (p. 4) or vegetable cooking water	500 mL
1 tbsp	Worcestershire sauce	15 mL
1 tsp	salt	5 mL
1 tbsp	minced fresh parsley	15 mL
½ tsp	dried thyme	2 mL
4 or 5	carrots, peeled and cut in 1-inch (2.5 cm) lengths	4 or 5
4 or 5	potatoes, peeled and cubed	4 or 5

Dredge meat in ¼ cup (50 mL) of flour and pepper. In large heavy kettle or Dutch oven, heat oil over medium heat; brown meat, in batches, until well seared.

Mince 1 of the onions; add to meat along with 2 cups (500 mL) of the tomato juice, stock, Worcestershire sauce, salt, parsley and thyme. Bring to boil; cover, reduce heat to low and simmer for 1½ to 2 hours or until meat is very tender. Add remaining onions, carrots and potatoes; cook for 30 to 40 minutes or until tender.

Stir remaining flour with remaining tomato juice. Add to stew and cook, stirring, for 2 to 3 minutes or until thickened. *Makes 6 to 8 servings.*

OLD-FASHIONED MEATLOAF

For the very best flavor, it's really important to use good medium lean ground beef for a meat loaf. Line your loaf pan with aluminum foil and lightly oil it. Serve with potatoes you've baked at the same time.

2 lb	medium ground beef	1 kg
1 or 2	onions, minced	1 or 2
2	eggs, lightly beaten	2
1 tbsp	grated horseradish	15 mL
1½ tsp	salt	7 mL
½ tsp	pepper	2 mL
1 cup	quick-cooking rolled oats or dry bread crumbs	250 mL
⅓ cup	ketchup (optional)	75 mL
1 to 2 tbsp	Worcestershire sauce	15 to 25 mL
1 or 2	carrots, grated Quick and Easy Barbecue Sauce (p. 29) (optional)	1 or 2

Preheat oven to 325°F (160°C).

In bowl and using hands, thoroughly blend beef, onions, eggs, horseradish, salt, pepper, oats, ketchup (if using), Worcestershire sauce and carrots. Pack into foil-lined greased 9- x 5-inch (2 L) loaf pan; cover lightly with foil.

Bake for 1½ to 2 hours or until edges are dark brown and pulling away from sides of pan, removing top foil during final 30 minutes of baking. Brush with barbecue sauce, if desired. Let stand for 10 minutes before lifting out of pan. Slice with sharp knife.

Makes 8 to 10 servings.

VARIATION:

For unexpected company, extend this recipe by layering meat with a mixture of 3 cups (750 mL) stale bread crumbs, 1 small minced onion, ½ tsp (2 mL) salt, ½ tsp (2 mL) ground sage and ¼ tsp (1 mL) pepper.

HUNGARIAN GOULASH WITH CARAWAY AND SOUR CREAM

There is no doubt that this is a family dish — not too expensive and quite stretchable. Add extra potatoes or serve it plain over steamed rice or a heap of buttery noodles.

4 to 6	slices side bacon	4 to 6
3 or 4	onions, minced	3 or 4
¼ cup	sweet Hungarian paprika	50 mL
½ tsp	caraway seeds, lightly crushed	2 mL
2 lb	round or chuck steak, sliced in thin strips	1 kg
2½ cups	chopped peeled tomatoes, fresh or canned	625 mL
	Salt and pepper	
2 or 3	potatoes, peeled and diced	2 or 3
	Sour cream or plain yoghurt	

In deep heavy skillet or Dutch oven, cook bacon until crisp. Remove and crumble; set aside.

Add onions to skillet; reduce heat to medium-low and cook until golden brown. Stir in paprika and caraway seeds; cook, stirring, for 10 to 15 seconds.

Add meat, stirring to coat evenly with paprika. Add 2 cups (500 mL) of the tomatoes; cover and simmer for 1 hour or until meat is almost tender. Season to taste with salt and pepper. Add potatoes; cook for 25 to 30 minutes or until meat and potatoes are tender.

Stir in reserved tomatoes and heat through. Place goulash in heated serving bowl; sprinkle with reserved bacon. Pass sour cream separately to dollop on each serving. *Makes 4 to 6 servings.*

FRIKADELLER
(DANISH MEAT PATTIES)
• •

A good friend, Nancy Knudstrup, makes this quick and easy supper dish quite regularly. She says that traditionally, it is served with Spicy Pickled Beets (p. 78), Peggy's Norwegian Cucumber Salad (p. 26), boiled potatoes and cooked red cabbage.

Although it calls for veal and pork, she often substitutes lean ground beef. If you don't have a meat grinder, ask your butcher to grind the veal and pork together.

½ lb	each boneless veal and pork	250 g
	OR	
1 lb	ground beef	500 g
3 tbsp	all-purpose flour	50 mL
1¼ cups	soda water	300 mL
	(one 10 oz/300 mL can)	
1	egg, well beaten	1
1 tsp	salt	5 mL
½ tsp	pepper	2 mL
2 tbsp	butter	25 mL
2 tbsp	vegetable oil	25 mL

Using finest blade of meat grinder, grind veal and pork together.

In large mixing bowl and using wooden spoon, beat flour into meat. Gradually beat in soda water until mixture is light and fluffy. Beat in egg, salt and pepper. Cover and refrigerate for 1 hour to allow mixture to become firm.

With moistened hands, shape meat mixture into oblong patties about 4 inches (10 cm) long. In large heavy skilled (preferably non-stick), heat butter and oil over medium heat; cook meat patties for 6 to 8 minutes per side or until well browned. Drain briefly on paper towels, if desired. Serve piping hot. *Makes 4 or 5 servings.*

CHEESEY
MACARONI AND BEEF SUPPER
••

S erve this quick dish with the fastest homemade bread I know
 how to make . . . a really healthy Whole Wheat Buttermilk Soda
Bread (p. 136). Enjoy!

¾ lb	lean ground beef	375 g
1 or 2	onions, diced	1 or 2
1	garlic clove, minced	1
1	can (28 oz/796 mL) tomatoes	1
2 tbsp	soy sauce	25 mL
1 tbsp	chili powder	25 mL
2 tsp	dried basil	10 mL
2 cups	uncooked macaroni or pasta shells	500 mL
1	medium zucchini, sliced	1
2 cups	shredded mozzarella, colby or Monterey Jack cheese	500 mL

Preheat oven to 350°F (180°C)

In large saucepan, brown beef, onions and garlic. Drain liquid from
tomatoes into measuring cup; add enough water to make 2½ cups
(625 mL). Add to saucepan along with tomatoes, soy sauce, chili
powder and basil; bring to boil. Stir in macaroni and zucchini.

Pour into well-greased 8-cup (2 L) baking dish. Bake, covered, for
25 minutes. Sprinkle with cheese. Bake, uncovered, for 15 minutes or
until cheese is bubbling and macaroni is tender but firm.

Makes 4 generous servings.

CRETONS
(QUEBEC'S ANSWER TO PÂTÉ)

This delicious old-fashioned meat spread is great on dark rye bread or simply sliced and placed on lettuce leaves. Store it for one or two days before eating to really develop its fullest flavors.

¼ lb	fatback pork, coarsely chopped	125 g
1½ lb	ground pork	750 g
½ cup	water	125 mL
⅓ cup	dry white wine	75 mL
1	medium onion, minced	1
2	garlic cloves, minced	2
½ tsp	ground cloves	2 mL
¾ tsp	pepper	4 mL
½ tsp	salt	2 mL

In large heavy saucepan, cook fatback pork, stirring often, for about 15 minutes or until browned and crispy. Remove fat and pork; set aside.

In same saucepan, combine ground pork, water and wine; simmer, uncovered, over very low heat for 1 hour, stirring occasionally. Add reserved pork fat and crisp pork chunks.

Stir in onion, garlic, cloves, pepper and salt. Cover and simmer gently over very low heat for 1 hour or until meat is tender. Let cool slightly; taste and adjust seasoning if needed.

Spoon into 9- x 5-inch (2 L) loaf pan or small individual pots. Cover tightly with plastic wrap and refrigerate until completely chilled. (Cretons may also be frozen for up to 1 month.) *Makes 8 to 10 servings.*

SPARERIBS WITH BUTTON
DUMPLINGS AND SAUERKRAUT

There are few country dishes that can equal spareribs and
sauerkraut. Serve this delicious version with Sourdough Dark
Rye Bread (p. 110).

3 to 4 lb	lean pork back spareribs, cut in pieces	1.5 to 2 kg
½ cup	water	125 mL
3 to 4 cups	sauerkraut	750 mL to 1 L
1 tsp	caraway seeds	5 mL
Button Dumplings:		
¾ cup	all-purpose flour	175 mL
¼ tsp	salt	1 mL
1½ tsp	baking powder	7 mL
1	egg	1
¼ cup	(approx) milk	50 mL

Preheat oven to 325°F (160°C).

In roasting pan, combine spareribs, water and sauerkraut including
juice and caraway; cover and roast for 3 to 3½ hours or until tender,
turning ribs halfway through cooking time. Remove ribs to platter and
keep warm.

Button Dumplings: Meanwhile, in bowl, stir together flour, salt and
baking powder; whisk in egg and enough milk to make stiff dough that
will hold its shape when dropped into sauerkraut.

Place roasting pan on top of stove. Add water if necessary to make
sauerkraut look quite wet; bring to boil over medium heat. Add small
spoonfuls of dumpling dough; cover tightly and cook for 12 minutes
without uncovering. Serve sauerkraut and dumplings around spareribs.

Makes 4 to 6 servings.

SWEET AND SOUR PORK CHOPS

The sauce for the chops is a standby in my kitchen. It can be used for other meats, too. Brown a pound or so of small meatballs or a rack of spareribs, cut into serving portions, then proceed with the recipe. Ladle over rice with chunks of pineapple and quickly sautéed green and red pepper folded in at the last moment.

4 to 6	lean loin or butt pork chops	4 to 6
	Vegetable oil	
1 or 2	garlic cloves, crushed	1 or 2
¾ tsp	ginger	4 mL
1 tsp	dry mustard	5 mL
¼ cup	granulated sugar	50 mL
2 tbsp	all-purpose flour	25 mL
3 tbsp	soy sauce	45 mL
3 tbsp	white vinegar	45 mL
1 cup	water	250 mL

Trim any excess fat from pork chops. In skillet, heat a little oil and brown chops quickly. Add garlic and sauté for a few minutes.

Meanwhile, in small bowl, stir together ginger, mustard, sugar and flour; whisk in soy sauce, vinegar and water. Add to skillet and bring to boil. Cover and simmer over low heat for 15 to 20 minutes or until meat is tender. *Makes 3 or 4 servings.*

GRILLED SMOKED PORK CHOPS WITH MUSTARDY MAPLE GLAZE

Fully cooked, smoked pork chops are available from many butchers and at farm markets across Canada. Fast and easy to prepare, they merely need a light brushing with a little oil and the following basting sauce before popping onto the barbecue or under the broiler.

Stir together about ⅓ cup (75 mL) maple syrup, 1 tbsp (15 mL) Dijon mustard and some horseradish. Brush over 6 to 8 smoked pork shops while grilling for 6 to 8 minutes or until warmed through and browned.

BAKED EASTER HAM LOAF

There is blue sky up behind all that gray. That's the way I feel after every winter and when Easter rolls around I know that spring can't be all that far behind.

The day lilies poke through, the tulips brave the cold nights and even the odd robin arrives home from winter vacation to bounce on the elderberry bush and wait for it to bloom.

Grind the remains of the Easter ham to make this delicious meat loaf with its sweet and sour glaze.

Meat Loaf:

1½ lb	ground ham	750 g
1 lb	ground raw pork	500 g
⅔ cup	bread crumbs	175 mL
½ cup	tomato juice or puréed tomatoes	125 mL
2	eggs, lightly beaten	2
½ tsp	salt (optional)	2 mL
½ tsp	pepper	2 mL

Sauce:

1 tbsp	brown sugar	15 mL
1 tsp	dry or Dijon mustard	5 mL
2 to 3 tbsp	water	25 to 50 mL
3 tbsp	cider vinegar	50 mL

Preheat oven to 350°F (180°C).

Meat Loaf: In large bowl, combine ham, pork and bread crumbs; mix thoroughly. Mix in tomato juice, eggs, salt (if using) and pepper. Form into loaf shape and place in lightly-oiled shallow baking pan.

Sauce: Stir together sugar, mustard, water and vinegar. Bake meat loaf for 1½ to 2 hours or until top begins to caramelize, basting with sauce 2 or 3 times during cooking. *Makes 8 to 10 servings.*

VARIATION:

My sister-in-law, Kay, often combines 3 tbsp (50 mL) dry mustard with ½ cup (125 mL) maple syrup to brush onto ham or loaves such as this one.

SPICY BARBECUED LAMB CHOPS

This basic recipe may also be used for marinating chunks of lean lamb prior to skewering for shish-kebabs. Substitute cumin, coriander, cardamom and curry powder for the 1 tbsp (15 mL) garam masala (a spice mixture readily found at most East Indian groceries) in the marinade if desired. The marinating time can vary from a few hours to two days . . . just turn the chops after a day, or if you have a leak-proof container, give it a shake.

12	lean loin lamb chops	12
1	small onion, minced	1
2	garlic cloves, minced	2
1 tsp	grated gingerroot	5 mL
1 tbsp	garam masala	15 mL
1½ tsp	curry powder	7 mL
¾ cup	light soy sauce	175 mL
¼ cup	vegetable or peanut oil	50 mL
½ cup	dry sherry	125 mL

Place lamb chops in marinating container. In bowl, mix together onion, garlic, ginger, garam masala, curry powder, soy sauce, oil and sherry; pour over chops. Cover tightly and refrigerate for at least 6 hours.

Remove chops from marinade and barbecue on greased grill over medium-hot coals for 2 to 3 minutes per side or until richly chestnut brown and still pink inside. *Makes 4 to 6 servings.*

FISH CAMP FISH FRY

· ·

All around the frozen lakes of northern Quebec and Ontario, wood-heated huts provide ice fishermen with shelter and a reason to have a good time. The fish that are caught run the gamut from lake trout to freshwater cod, sometimes known as "lotte."

The lotte I had from those gravel-bottomed lakes was sweet and delicious. It had been skinned and marinated overnight before it was cooked and the sacs of roe were also breaded and fried in butter.

This same marinade can be used for any freshwater fish. Sylvie Larouche, the lady who told me about this method, says she uses it for trout and pickerel as well. Serve with hot mashed potatoes, Old-Fashioned Coleslaw (p. 24) and beer.

4 or 5	onions, thinly sliced	4 or 5
2 to 3 lb	whitefish fillets, skinned if necessary and cut into serving pieces	1 to 1.5 kg
2 cups	vegetable oil	500 mL
1 tsp	salt	5 mL
½ tsp	pepper	2 mL
2	eggs, beaten	2
½ tsp	salt	2 mL
¼ tsp	pepper	1 mL
2 cups	finely ground dry bread crumbs	500 mL
	Butter or vegetable oil	

In glass or ceramic container, layer onions and fish. Whisk together oil, salt and pepper; pour over mixture. Cover and refrigerate for 12 hours.

Remove fish from marinade; pat dry with paper towels. Set marinade aside. Whisk together eggs, salt and pepper.

Dip fish into egg mixture, then into bread crumbs.

In skillet, heat butter over medium heat; fry fish until deep golden, 4 to 5 minutes per side. Remove and keep warm in foil. With slotted spoon, remove onions from marinade and cook quickly in separate skillet until golden. *Makes 8 to 10 servings.*

LAKE HURON WHITEFISH FILLETS
WITH TOASTY CHEESE TOPPING

L ong gone are the days when a "fish man" came door to door in our rural neighborhood just north of Toronto. Finding great fish can still sometimes be a difficult task in the Great Lakes region, but if you are lucky enough to have a fresh source of splake, whitefish or trout, here's an excellent recipe. It's similar to having a cheese bread crust all over the delicate flesh.

2 lb	fresh fish fillets	1 kg
½ tsp	salt	2 mL
	Pepper	
⅓ cup	butter	75 mL
1 or 2	medium onions, diced	1 or 2
1½ tsps	dry mustard	7 mL
3 cups	croutons or bread crumbs, toasted	750 mL
1 cup	shredded medium Cheddar cheese	250 mL
2 tbsp	minced fresh parsley	25 mL

Preheat oven to 350°F (180°C).

In lightly greased 13- x 9-inch (3.5 L) baking dish, sprinkle fillets with salt and pepper to taste; set aside.

In large skillet, melt butter over medium heat; cook onions until tender, 4 to 5 minutes. Stir in mustard, croutons, cheese and parsley, tossing to combine completely. Spread over fish and bake, uncovered, for 25 to 30 minutes or until fish is opaque and flakes easily when tested with fork. *Makes 6 to 8 servings.*

BARBECUED TROUT

In anticipation of a feast of fresh rainbow trout, here is a fish-barbecuing recipe. Serve with tartar sauce or simply lemon slices.

4	rainbow trout	4
	Salt and pepper	
4 to 8	sprigs fresh thyme	4 to 8
4	green onions	4
¼ cup	chopped fresh parsley	50 mL
	Olive oil	

Clean trout, leaving heads on if desired; dry well. Sprinkle inside and out with salt and pepper. Stuff cavities with thyme, onions and parsley. Close with small metal skewers. Brush fish lightly with oil.

On greased grill over medium-hot heat, close lid and cook trout for 4 to 5 minutes on each side or until flesh is opaque. *Makes 4 servings.*

SAVING THE HARVEST — PICKLES, PRESERVES AND HERBS

INTRODUCTION TO PRESERVING

Making pickles and preserves is as exacting an art as cake baking. Being slap-dash about it can actually kill you. Botulism has no favorites and hence sterilization and final processing are of utmost importance.

Prepare all vegetables and fruits by washing them in cool water to remove garden dirt. Make sure that your counter, tea towels, spoons and other utensils are sparkling clean and dry.

Use jars with properly fitted lids. Discard used Mason jar lids from year to year. Any dented jar rings should be replaced. Never use jars that don't have two-part lids.

To Sterilize Glass Jars:

Place well-washed, rinsed but not dried jars on shallow metal try in 225°F (110°C) oven for 15 minutes. Turn off oven and leave jars in oven until filling. Handle carefully when removing and set on kitchen towels before and during filling.

Sterilize metal lids for 5 minutes in boiling water or glass lids in oven with jars.

The Boiling Water Bath

This method of sterilization ensures the safety and shelf life of your preserves and pickles. It cannot be used to can meat, fish or low acid vegetables like corn, peas or beans.

These general instructions may be used for any of the recipes in this chapter. You will need a large canning kettle made of enamelware, which is also called "granite." It is fitted with a rack to hold jars and has a loose-fitting lid. It must be deep enough to hold jars and allow them to be covered by 1 inch (2.5 cm) boiling water.

Prepare food to be canned and fill sterilized jars, leavin ½-inch (1 cm) headspace at top. Wipe off any drips around rim of jars. Attach lids according to manufacturer's instructions.

Place canner on stove. Pour in cool water until it reaches about one-third up side of kettle. Turn on heat and allow water to become quite hot. Lower jars into it with tongs and add enough hot water to cover the lids by 2 inches (5 cm). There should be enough space between jars for the boiling water to circulate freely. Cover and bring the water to a boil over medium-high heat. Begin timing when the water begins to boil.

After required amount of time (see individual recipe), remove jars carefully using tongs. Set on a kitchen towel and let cool before storing in a cold room or refrigerator.

MOM'S
BREAD-AND-BUTTER PICKLES

I eat these pickles with cold roast beef on homemade brown bread. The flecks of sweet red pepper make them a particularly attractive pickle.

3 quarts	medium-sized cucumbers	3 L
2 to 3 cups	sliced peeled small onions	500 to 750 mL
⅔ cup	minced red sweet pepper	150 mL
⅓ cup	minced green sweet pepper	75 mL
Brine:		
8 cups	hot water	2 L
1 cup	coarse pickling salt	250 mL
Pickling Liquid:		
6 cups	white vinegar	1.5 L
3 cups	granulated sugar	750 mL
1½ tsp	turmeric	7 mL
1 tsp	mustard seeds	5 mL
1 tsp	celery seeds	5 mL

Scrub and thinly slice cucumbers without peeling. In large glass bowl, toss cucumbers with onions, red and green pepper.

Brine: Combine hot water with salt; pour over vegetables. Let stand, covered, for 3 hours; drain thoroughly.

Pickling Liquid: In large saucepan, combine vinegar, sugar, turmeric, mustard and celery seeds; bring to boil over medium-high heat. Add vegetables and return to boil. Immediately remove from heat. Ladle into hot, sterilized 2-cup (500 mL) jars. Leaving ½-inch (1 cm) headspace, attach the lids according to manufacturer's directions. Process in a boiling-water bath (p. 74) for 10 minutes. Let cool at room temperature before refrigerating or storing in cool, dark place for up to 1 year. *Makes 16 to 18 cups (4 to 4.5 L).*

MOM'S ICICLE PICKLES

I remember when we were given a jar and this recipe by a lawyer's wife in Mount Forest, Ontario. I was in Grade 11. Since then, the identical recipe has popped up all across Canada. It has won at least two ribbons in Ontario fall fairs because it is everything a pickle should be — crisp and green with a pungent, sweet-sour flavor.

Choose small- to medium-sized cucumbers and make sure that they are really fresh.

6 quarts	young firm cucumbers	6 L
12 cups	cold water	3 L
2 cups	coarse pickling salt	500 mL
1 tbsp	alum	15 mL
Syrup:		
16 cups	granulated sugar	4 L
12 cups	white vinegar	3 L
½ cup	whole mixed pickling spice, tied in cheesecloth bag	125 mL

Wash and cut cucumbers into long thin strips. Place in 8-cup (2 L) crock or very large glass or ceramic container.

In saucepan, bring water and salt to boil; pour over cucumbers. Cover and place crock in cool place for 6 days, stirring every day.

Pour off brine; cover with fresh boiling water and let stand for 24 hours.

Drain cucumbers; cover with more boiling water mixed with alum. Let stand for 24 hours. Drain.

Syrup: In large kettle, combine sugar, vinegar and pickling spice; bring to boil and pour over cucumbers. Let stand for 1 day. Drain and return syrup to boil; pour over pickles. Repeat three times for a total of 4 days. Remove cheesecloth bag. Pack into sterilized jars. Leaving ½ -inch (1 cm) headspace; seal jars.

Process in boiling-water bath (p. 74) for 10 minutes. Let cool at room temperature before refrigerating or storing in cook, dark place for up to 1 year. *Makes 24 to 32 cups (6 to 8 L).*

SPICY PICKLED BEETS

This recipe has been in my family for as long as I can remember. My parents make them together . . . an afternoon of cooking with each other. Dad's jars are usually filled with large chunks of beets, while my Mother's are tiny and perfectly packed. I love them both.

2 or 3	bunches of beets, scrubbed and tops removed	2 or 3
	Cinnamon sticks	
1½ cups	white vinegar	375 mL
½ cup	water	125 mL
¾ cup	granulated sugar	175 mL
1 tbsp	pickling salt	15 mL
1 tsp	cinnamon	5 mL
1 tsp	ground allspice	5 mL
1 tsp	whole cloves	5 mL

In large pot of boiling water, cook beets until tender, 15 to 20 minutes for large beets, 10 to 15 minutes for small. Drain and rinse under cold water. Peel off skins. Pack beets into sterilized jars along with cinnamon stick into each 2-cup (500 mL) jar.

In heavy saucepan, combine vinegar, water, sugar, salt, cinnamon, allspice and cloves; bring to full boil. Pour immediately over beets. Run knife around beets carefully to dislodge any bubbles. Leaving ½-inch (1 cm) headspace. Seal jars. Process in boiling-water bath (p. 74) for 30 minutes. Let cool at room temperature before refrigerating or storing in cool, dark place for up to 1 year. *Makes 8 to 10 cups (2 to 2.5 L).*

THE CHILI SAUCE RECIPE

L istening to the radio last fall, it would appear that when cooks make chili sauce, they automatically think that theirs is the very best recipe ever . . . or at the very least, their mother's is. I beg to differ. My mother and I have been perfuming our autumnal homes with the rich smell of simmering tomatoes for decades and THIS is the ultimate recipe. If there is one trick, it's having a heavy enough kettle to simmer the sweetened sauce for the length of time that it takes to thicken it without scorching. Before ladling into jars, remember to keep a bowl out for yourself to go with tomorrow morning's scrambled eggs and toast.

The amount of sugar will vary from year to year depending on the acidity of the tomatoes . . . it's simply a matter of taste.

6 quarts	ripe tomatoes	6 L
3	large onions, minced	3
½ cup	coarse pickling salt	125 mL
3 cups	diced celery	750 mL
2	large sweet red peppers, seeded and diced	2
⅓ cup	whole mixed pickling spice, tied in cheesecloth bag	75 mL
¾ tsp	red pepper flakes	4 mL
1½ cups	apple cider vinegar	375 mL
4 cups	brown sugar	1 L

Peel and slice tomatoes into large bowl. Add onions and salt. Cover and let stand overnight or at least 8 hours. Drain thoroughly and place into heavy saucepan.

Stir in celery, red peppers, pickling spice, red pepper flakes and vinegar; cover and bring to boil over medium heat. Uncover and simmer over low heat for at least 2 hours or until thickened, stirring often to prevent sticking.

Add brown sugar. Taste and adjust seasonings if necessary. Simmer for 25 minutes or until thickened once again. Remove cheesecloth bag. Ladle into hot sterilized jars, leaving ½ -inch (1 cm) headspace; seal jars. Process in boiling water bath (p. 74) for 10 minutes. Let cool at room temperature before refrigerating or storing in a cool, dark place for up to 1 year.

Makes 12 to 14 cups (3 to 3.5 mL).

RAW CHILI SAUCE

T ry this with everything from omelettes to grilled cheese sandwiches. To a cook, making this relish is what planting zucchini is to a gardener: it simply never fails.

6 quarts	ripe tomatoes, peeled	6 L
2	bunches celery, finely diced	2
12	medium onions, minced	12
1 or 2	hot peppers, seeded and minced	1 or 2
2	sweet red peppers, seeded and minced	2
1 cup	coarse pickling salt	250 mL
4½ cups	cider vinegar	1.125 L
8 cups	granulated sugar	2 L
2 tsp	mustard seeds	10 mL
1 tsp	cinnamon	5 mL
1 tsp	ginger	5 mL
1 tsp	ground cloves	5 mL

Chop tomatoes finely and place in large glass or crockery bowl. Add celery, onions, hot and sweet peppers and salt; stir to mix well. Cover and let stand overnight. Drain, pressing out any excess juice.

In large saucepan, combine vinegar, sugar, mustard seeds, cinnamon, ginger and cloves; bring to rapid boil, stirring to dissolve sugar. Add vegetables and stir. Immediately ladle into sterilized 2-cup (500 mL) jars, leaving ½ -inch (1 cm) headspace. Seal.

Process in boiling-water bath (p. 74) for 15 minutes. Let cool at room temperature before refrigerating or storing in cool, dark place for up to 1 year. *Makes 20 to 24 cups (5 to 6 L).*

MOTHER MAYNE'S MUSTARD PICKLE

There are good pickle makers and there are pickle makers without peer. It has to do with patience, I'm sure. After raising nine children, Elaine Mayne has acquired the patience to make her a great pickle maker.

This is the best mustard pickle recipe I have ever come across. The secret is in the careful chopping of the cucumbers and onions: they should be in even ½-inch (1 cm) chunks. When properly made, the coarse relish is great on everything from barbecued hamburgers to scrambled eggs.

2 quarts	small fresh cucumbers, washed and chopped in ½-inch (1 cm) chunks	2 L
1 quart	onions, peeled and chopped in ½-inch (1 cm) chunks.	1 L
2 tbsp	coarse pickling salt	25 mL
1	large sweet green pepper, seeded and chopped finely	1
1	large sweet red pepper, seeded and chopped finely	1
2	stalks celery, diced	2
4 cups	white vinegar	1 L
5 cups	granulated sugar	1.25 L
¾ cup	all-purpose flour	175 mL
1 tbsp	dry mustard	15 mL
1 tsp	turmeric	5 mL

In glass or crockery bowl, combine cucumbers and onions; sprinkle with salt. Cover and let stand overnight.

Drain well and place in heavy pot; add green and red peppers, celery, vinegar and sugar. Cover and bring to boil; reduce heat and simmer for 10 minutes.

Meanwhile, stir together flour, mustard and turmeric; pour in some of the boiling liquid, stirring to prevent lumps. Return entire mixture to pot and bring to boil; cook for 1 to 2 minutes or until thickened.

Ladle into sterilized 2 cup (500 mL) jars, leaving ½-inch (1 cm) headspace. Seal. Process in boiling-water bath (p. 74) for 15 minutes.. Let cool at room temperature before storing in the refrigerator or a cool, dark place for up to 1 year. *Makes 8 to 10 cups (2 to 2.5 L).*

KAY'S ULTIMATE HOT DOG
AND HAMBURGER RELISH

M y sister-in-law, Kay, is a great cook. I don't think there's anything much better than a charcoal-grilled burger on a homemade bun with her relish, some fried onions and a bit of mustard.

If you have an extra zucchini, substitute it for one or two of the cucumbers.

8	large cucumbers	8
18	green tomatoes, stemmed	18
4	sweet green peppers, seeded	4
2	sweet red peppers, seeded	2
1 or 2	hot red peppers, seeded	1 or 2
6	large onions	6
½ cup	coarse pickling salt	125 mL
	White vinegar	
1 cup	finely diced celery	250 mL
7 cups	granulated sugar	1.75 L
½ cup	all-purpose flour	125 mL
2 tbsp	dry mustard	25 mL
1 tsp	turmeric	5 mL
¼ cup	cold water	50 mL

Wash cucumbers, tomatoes, green, red and hot peppers. Peel onions. Grind vegetables into large plastic or glass bowl; sprinkle with salt. Cover and let stand overnight.

Drain off juice. Transfer vegetables to large heavy saucepan. Pour in enough vinegar to just cover surface of relish; add celery. Stir in sugar and bring to boil over medium heat, stirring frequently. Cover, reduce heat and simmer for 20 minutes.

In jar, shake together flour, mustard, turmeric and water; stir into boiling relish and cook, stirring constantly, until thickened, 5 to 10 minutes. Ladle into hot sterilized jars, leaving ½-inch (1 cm) headspace; seal. Process in boiling-water bath (p. 74) for 10 minutes. Let cool at room temperature before storing in either the refrigerator or a cool, dark place for up to 1 year. *Makes 30 to 32 cups (7.5 to 8 L).*

ELEANOR'S GREEN TOMATO PICKLE

This is a modernized version of an old recipe which used to be called "Governor's Sauce." Recipes such as this are traditional throughout most of our provinces. In Quebec, it was served with tourtière. In my grandparents' kitchen, it was served with roasted meats. When I was a child, a few dusky-colored jars of the old-fashioned version were always in our fruit cellar.

8 cups	chopped or sliced green tomatoes	2 L
2	large onions, diced	2
1	large sweet green pepper, seeded and chopped	1
¼ cup	coarse pickling salt	50 mL
1½ cups	white vinegar	375 mL
1½ cups	granulated sugar	375 mL
2 tsp	mustard seeds	10 mL
1½ tsp	celery seeds	7 mL
1 tsp	cinnamon	5 mL
¼ tsp	turmeric	1 mL

In large glass or crockery bowl, combine tomatoes, onions and green pepper. Sprinkle with salt and stir. Cover and let stand for 2 hours. Drain and rinse thoroughly under cold running water. Drain again.

In heavy saucepan, combine vinegar, sugar, mustard seeds, celery seeds, cinnamon and turmeric; bring to boil over medium heat. Stir in drained vegetables and return to boil. Reduce heat and simmer, uncovered, for 15 minutes, stirring constantly. Ladle into sterilized 2-cup (500 mL) jars, leaving ½-inch (1 cm) headspace. Seal. Process in boiling water bath (p. 74) for 10 minutes. Let cool at room temperature before refrigerating or storing in cool, dark place. *Makes 8 cups (2 L).*

ARTHUR TOWNSHIP
GREEN TOMATO MINCEMEAT
••

This is another recipe that has it roots in a cold northern climate where tomatoes don't always reach their peak of juicy ripeness. I freeze the mincemeat in 2-cup (500 mL) margarine tubs . . . two containers make a 10-inch (25 cm) pie. Try using Ida Red or Northern Spy apples. It's superb!

15 cups	finely chopped green tomatoes	3.75 L
20 cups	water	5 L
5 cups	chopped tart apples	1.25 L
½ lb	ground suet*	250 g
2 ½ lb	brown sugar	1.25 kg
1 lb	sultana raisins	500 g
1 cup	cider vinegar	250 mL
½ lb	mixed candied peel	250 g
	Salt	
1 tbsp	cinnamon	15 mL
1 tbsp	ground cloves	15 mL
1 tbsp	grated nutmeg	15 mL

Drain chopped tomatoes thoroughly and place in large heavy saucepan; add water and bring to boil over medium heat. Cover and simmer for 1 hour. Remove from heat and let stand overnight.

Drain tomatoes thoroughly; return to heavy saucepan. Add apples, suet, sugar, raisins, vinegar and peel. Taste and season with salt if desired.

Bring to boil over medium heat; reduce heat to low and simmer gently for 2 hours, stirring often. Stir in cinnamon, cloves and nutmeg; cook for 10 minutes. Ladle into hot sterilized jars and seal. Process in boiling-water bath (p. 74) for 25 minutes, or simply refrigerate for up to 2 months. *Makes about 12 cups (3 L).*

*Instead of suet, butter or margarine may be dabbed onto the pies just before baking.

GINGER PEACH CHUTNEY

Since markets and roadside stands have always been a weakness with me, there are always baskets of fresh fruit and vegetables sitting on the kitchen floor in various stages of fermentation.

It would be sin to waste any of this great produce, so I dig out my old red binder full of my favorite recipes and usually make at least a half-dozen kinds of pickles.

7 cups	sliced peeled fresh peaches	1.75 mL
2 tbsp	coarse pickling salt	25 mL
3 cups	granulated sugar (or part brown)	750 mL
1 ½ cups	cider vinegar	375 mL
3	large cloves garlic, minced	3
1 cup	minced onion	250 mL
1½ tsp	ginger	7 mL
½ tsp	red pepper flakes	2 mL
¾ cup	lemon juice	175 mL
1 cup	sultana or golden raisins	250 mL
½ cup	chopped candied ginger (or more)	125 mL

In large bowl, cover peaches with brine of the coarse salt and 4 cups (1 L) water. Let stand overnight. Drain thoroughly.

In large saucepan, combine ¼ cup (50 L) water, sugar, cider vinegar and garlic; bring to boil. Add peaches; cover and simmer until fruit is translucent. With slotted spoon, remove peaches from syrup and set aside.

Add onion, ginger, red pepper flakes, lemon juice and raisins to saucepan; cook, uncovered, until thickened, 15 to 20 minutes. Add peaches and ginger; return to boil. Immediately ladle into hot sterilized jars. Seal and store in cool, dark place.

Makes 6 to 8 cups (1.5 to 2 L).

HOT PEPPER JELLY

We love this jelly with meats and cheeses. Use the freshest hot peppers you can find but handle them carefully and use rubber gloves when seeding and chopping. If you can, use the food processor both to speed things up as well as protect your skin.

12	hot red peppers	12
	3 to 4 inch (8 to 10 cm) long	
¼ cup	cider vinegar	50 mL
6 cups	granulated sugar	1.5 L
1 cup	white vinegar	250 mL
1	bottle (170 mL) liquid pectin	1

Wash and seed peppers; chop finely.

In large heavy saucepan, combine peppers, cider vinegar, sugar and white vinegar; cover and bring to boil over medium heat, stirring often.

Increase heat to high; pour in pectin. Boil hard for 1 minute. Remove from heat. With metal spoon, stir and skim for 4 to 5 minutes to cool and prevent peppers from floating.

Ladle into sterilized jars and seal. *Makes 5 cups (1.25 L).*

CHUNKY PEACH CONSERVE

I have used both peaches and apricots for this delicious preserve. It makes a superb hostess gift, if it makes it that far.

3 cups	diced peeled peaches	750 mL
6 ½ cups	granulated sugar	1.625 L
2 ½ cups	mashed peeled peaches	625 mL
¼ cup	lemon juice	50 mL
1	bottle (170 mL) liquid pectin	1
1 cup	chopped drained maraschino cherries	250 mL
⅓ cup	blanched slivered almonds	75 mL
⅓ cup	diced candied ginger	75 mL

In large heavy saucepan, combine diced peaches with 1 cup (250 mL) of the sugar; bring to boil over medium heat. Reduce heat to low and simmer, covered, until tender, 4 to 5 minutes. Add remaining sugar, mashed peaches and lemon juice; stir well.

Bring to full rolling boil over medium-high heat; boil hard for 1 minute, stirring constantly. Pour in pectin; boil for 1 minute, stirring. Remove from heat.

Add cherries, almonds and ginger. With metal spoon, stir and skim for 5 minutes to cool slightly and prevent fruit from floating. Ladle into hot sterilized jars and seal. Store in cool, dark place.

Makes 7 to 8 cups (1.75 to 2 L).

ELDERBERRY SYRUP

•••••••••••••••••••••••••••••••

M y father remembers his mother making this syrup from the plentiful elderberries that used to flourish along the back roads of Central Ontario. It is delicious on pancakes or — for a real treat — stir a few spoonfuls into a glass of cold milk.

You can make chokecherry syrup the same way, but reduce the sugar to equal the amount of measured juice.

6 cups	stemmed elderberries	1.5 L
6 cups	water	1.5 L
12 cups	granulated sugar	3 L
¼ cup	lemon juice	50 mL

In large saucepan, combine berries and water; cover and bring to boil over medium heat. Reduce heat and simmer for 20 to 30 minutes or until fruit is very soft. Transfer to dampened jelly bag or colander lined with several layers of cheesecloth. Let drip into basin or large bowl overnight.

Measure 6 cups (1.5 L) of the juice into large heavy saucepan. Stir in sugar and lemon juice. Cook over low heat, stirring, until sugar has dissolved. Increase heat to high and bring to boil; cook, stirring, for 5 minutes or until syrupy. Pour into sterilized jars and seal.

Makes about 10 cups (2.5 L).

WELLINGTON COUNTY
WILD GRAPE JELLY
••••••••••••••••••••••••••••••

Grape picking can be tricky: first you need to find them. Check along hedgerows, in abandoned orchards, near old fences and especially lovers' lanes. Then, scissors in hand and well covered with bug repellent, you have to free the sometimes sparse clusters from the convoluted vines. When I remember to take them, I wear garden gloves.

Slathered on hot biscuits, wild grape jelly is so incredible that it will make you wonder whether you've ever tasted the flavor "grape" before. We also like it with meats such as farmers' sausage and breaded pork chops.

3 lb	wild grapes, stemmed	1.5 kg
3 cups	water	750 mL
4½ cups	granulated sugar	1.125 L
Half	bottle (170 mL) liquid pectin	Half

In large heavy saucepan, crush grapes with potato masher. Add water and bring to boil. Reduce heat and simmer, covered, for 15 to 20 minutes or until fruit is very tender. Transfer to dampened jelly bag or colander lined with double layer of cheesecloth (J-cloths work perfectly). Let drip into large pan overnight.

Measure 3 cups (750 mL) juice into large saucepan. Stir in sugar and mix well. Bring to boil over high heat, stirring constantly. Pour in pectin and bring to full rolling boil; boil hard for 1 minute, stirring constantly.

Remove from heat. With metal spoon, stir and skim off foam. Pour into sterilized jars and seal. Store in cool, dark place.

Makes about 5 cups (1.25 L).

JEFF'S LEMONADE CONCENTRATE

M y son Jeff came home from a summer job in the Rockies
raving about his friend Rosemary's lemonade. This is her
recipe, well tried and very good — just the thing to take the edge off a
mountain-climbing thirst.

3	large lemons	3
5 cups	boiling water	1.25 L
2 oz	citric acid*	56 g
5 cups	granulated sugar	1.25 L

Peel yellow rind off lemons; place in blender. Cut white pith away
from lemon and discard. Chop pulp and add to blender. Pour in 1 cup
(250 mL) of the boiling water; process for 1 to 2 minutes or until
thoroughly liquefied.

In large bowl, mix together remaining boiling water, citric acid and
sugar. Add lemon mixture; cover and let stand overnight.

Pour through sieve into glass jar. Refrigerate until needed. To serve,
put 2 to 3 tbsp (25 to 50 mL) syrup into glass and fill with ice water.

Makes 6 cups (1.5 L).

* Citric acid is available at most drug stores.

PESTO
· · · · · · · · · ·

Freezing fresh herbs is probably the simplest and most effective way of keeping them handy for the winter. Wash the leaves and pat dry. Layer them in small plastic bags and squeeze out the air. Secure with a twist tie and pop into the deep freeze.

You can also make fresh herb jellies, preserve herbs in vinegar or freeze this delicious Italian sauce, pesto, to serve later over Herbed Egg Pasta (p. 45).

To serve this pesto, add ½ cup (125 mL) grated Parmesan cheese and toss with freshly cooked hot pasta.

Parsley may be substituted for part of the basil. Try thyme with hazelnuts or cilantro with peanuts.

3	garlic cloves	3
2 cups	packed basil leaves	500 mL
⅓ cup	pine nuts or walnuts	75 mL
1 tsp	salt	5 mL
½ tsp	pepper	2 mL
¾ cup	olive oil	175 mL

In blender or food processor, process garlic, basil, pine nuts, salt and pepper until finely chopped. With machine still running, gradually pour in oil and purée. Scrape into freezer container. Seal and freeze for up to 6 months. Makes about 1 cup (250 mL).

FRESH HERB VINEGARS
· ·

This general method can be used for any variety of herbs. Pack a large jar with fresh, clean herb leaves. Cover with a good-quality white wine or rice wine vinegar. Do not use the ordinary white vinegar as it is far too overpowering. Cover and leave in a cool, dark place for a few weeks. Strain into small, decorative bottles. Drop in a sprig of the corresponding herb if available and seal. Store in a cool, dark place.

FRESH FRUIT PURÉE FOR DESSERTS

You can taste the summer sun in these easy purées, ready to pool under your favorite dessert. I use any really ripe fruit that is in season . . . blackberries or salmonberries if I'm in British Columbia . . . Saskatoons or blueberries if I'm on the Prairies . . . more blueberries here in Ontario or in Quebec . . . our superb wild raspberries or pitted cherries . . . peaches, apricots . . . it's endless.

If the fruit is frozen at its peak of ripeness, then the thawed product, although it'll be a little runny, will have a flavor as close to summer as you can get.

If the fruit is soft enough to purée without cooking, simply chop, purée and sweeten with sugar or local honey. It's difficult to imagine a better purée than wild trailing blackberries sweetened with delicate fireweed honey.

In the winter, I find it best to sweeten the fruit as it thaws and partially cooks on the stove. Don't cook it too much, just heat until thawed enough to pass through a food mill.

If you are using peaches or pears, which discolor, add a little fresh lemon juice, then sweeten appropriately.

Use a food mill or purée the fruit in a blender or food processor. To remove the seeds from raspberries or the like, pass the purée through a sieve.

Refrigerate, covered, until needed.

A fresh fruit purée should keep for 5 to 7 days. Freeze if desired.

FRESH MINT TEA

On Manitoulin Island in Ontario, the Nishnabe ("council of the three fires") people harvest their mint in the summertime to have all year round. Mary Lou Fox, of the Odawa band, says that to identify it properly, you look for a square stem. It grows in profusion all over the island.

To make wild mint tea, simply pour boiling water over several handfuls of fresh mint in a teapot. I pack mine about half-full of leaves. Allow it to steep for 4 to 5 minutes before serving. Wildflower honey is lovely with it, as is the completely non-traditional squeeze of lemon.

HEARTY BREAKFASTS

TOASTED HAZELNUT
WAFFLES WITH MAPLE SYRUP

In the very early spring (so early that it's really still winter), the hardwood forests all over Waterloo and Wellington counties of Ontario have curls of steam and smoke rising as the "sugaring off" begins. The first-run syrup is like nectar. The pioneers liked it so much that they would dip their homemade white bread into it as a springtime dessert. We like it poured over pancakes and waffles.

As the season progresses and the weather warms, the syrup darkens and for some reason, it becomes less expensive. I prefer this dark, almost coffee-colored syrup because it has the heartiest maple flavor.

Sadly, because of acid rain, our maple forests are diminishing. Enjoy this wonderful local product now, while we have it because someday it really will be an "old-fashioned" treat.

Roast about ¾ cup (175 mL) whole hazelnuts in a 350°F (160°C) oven for 10 to 15 minutes. Cool, rub off the loosened skins with your hands or between two layers of towelling then grind either in a mortar and pestle or in a processor.

1¼ cups	milk	300 mL
¼ cup	vegetable oil	50 mL
2	eggs, separated	2
1 cup	unbleached all-purpose flour	250 mL
½ cup	ground toasted hazelnuts	125 mL
1 tbsp	brown sugar	15 mL
	Maple syrup	

In large bowl, whisk together milk, oil and egg yolks. In separate bowl, beat egg whites until stiff; set aside. Stir together flour, nuts and sugar; whisk into milk mixture. Fold in egg whites.

Heat waffle iron over medium heat; brush with a little oil and pour in about ½ cup (125 mL) batter. Cook for 1 minute; flip and cook for 1½ minutes or until deep golden on bottom. Repeat with remaining batter. Serve with maple syrup. *Makes about 12 waffles.*

GOLDEN WHOLE WHEAT WAFFLES

These waffles are great served warm with fresh berries or other ripe, seasonal fruits and, of course, maple syrup. Although I usually make them in the food processor, they are just as easily whisked together in a large bowl.

¾ cup	unbleached all-purpose flour	175 mL
¼ cup	whole wheat or buckwheat flour	50 mL
½ tsp	baking powder	2 mL
2 tbsp	granulated sugar	25 mL
2	eggs	2
1 cup	milk	250 mL
1 tbsp	vegetable oil or melted better	15 mL

In food processor, combine all-purpose flour, whole wheat flour, baking powder and sugar; process with on-and-off motion just to blend. With machine running, add eggs, milk and oil; process just until batter is smooth. Let stand for 20 to 30 minutes at room temperature before using. (If weather is very warm, refrigerate batter.)

Heat lightly greased waffle iron over medium heat; pour in batter in batches and cook for about 3 minutes, turning after 1 minute, or until waffles are crisp and golden. *Makes 3 or 4 servings.*

BREAKFAST CRÊPES

Especially in strawberry season, we love eating these crêpes filled and topped with fresh sweet berries, sour cream (the light variety is fine) and a drizzle of maple syrup. If you're not going to eat the crêpes right away, cover and refrigerate them. Then reheat by flopping back, one at a time, on to a hot skillet or crêpe pan.

1½ cups	all-purpose flour	375 mL
2 tbsp	granulated sugar	25 mL
½ tsp	salt	2 mL
2 cups	milk	500 mL
4	eggs	4
¼ cup	butter, melted	50 mL

In large bowl, stir together flour, sugar and salt. Vigorously whisk in milk, eggs and butter. (Alternatively, combine dry ingredients in blender or food processor. With machine running, add milk, eggs and butter. Process, scraping sides down once or twice, until batter is smooth and velvety.) Let batter stand for 30 minutes before using.

Heat lightly greased crêpe pan or skillet over medium heat; pour in about 3 tbsp (50 mL) batter for each crêpe. Tilt and swirl pan to spread batter evenly. Cook for 1 to 2 minutes or until bottom is golden and edges begin to lift. Flip and cook for 10 to 15 seconds only.

Makes 18 crêpes.

GOLDEN CHEESE BLINTZES

For a spectacular dessert presentation, garnish each plate with fresh fruit and small dollops of sour cream swirled into the purée.

½ cup	golden raisins	125 mL
¼ cup	dark rum	50 mL
1 lb	cream cheese	500 g
1 lb	creamed cottage cheese	500 g
2	egg yolks	2
¼ cup	granulated sugar	50 mL
	Grated rind of 1 lemon	
¼ tsp	grated nutmeg	1 mL
8	Breakfast Crêpes (p. 98)	8
	Unsalted butter as needed	
2⅔ cups	Fresh Fruit Purée (p. 93), optional	650 mL
	Icing sugar	

In bowl, combine raisins and rum; let soak overnight or all day. Drain. Preheat oven to 400°F (200°C).

In large mixing bowl, beat together cream cheese, cottage cheese and egg yolks. Still beating, add sugar, lemon rind, nutmeg and drained raisins. Divide among crêpes and fold crêpes over filling into small pillow shapes.

In heavy skillet, sauté blintzes in butter until golden. Transfer to baking sheet and bake for 10 minutes or until thoroughly heated through. Serve immediately or pour about ⅓ cup (75 mL) Fruit Purée onto each serving plate and top with one blintz. Dust tops with icing sugar. *Makes 8 servings.*

BUCKWHEAT CRÊPES

· ·

B uckwheat, or sarazzin, was one of the first grains that the settlers
planted when they came to Canada. In Quebec, buckwheat
grew where many grains wouldn't have survived.

To serve the crêpes, fill with stir-fried vegetables that have been
blended with a little sour cream, or apples that have been poached in
maple syrup or simply like a Paris street vendor — a handful of grated
cheese liberally seasoned with black pepper.

⅔ cup	all-purpose flour (preferably unbleached)	150 mL
⅓ cup	buckwheat flour	75 mL
1¼ cups	milk or buttermilk	300 mL
2	eggs	2
2 tbsp	vegetable oil	25 mL

In food processor, blender or bowl, combine all-purpose and
buckwheat flours. Add milk, eggs and oil; process or vigorously whisk
until blended. Let stand for 20 minutes before using.

Heat lightly greased crêpe pan or skillet over medium heat; pour in
about ¼ cup (50 mL) batter per crêpe. Tilt and swirl pan to spread
batter evenly. Cook for 1 to 2 minutes or until bottom is golden and
edges begin to lift. Flip and cook for 10 to 15 seconds.

Makes about 16 crêpes.

BUCKWHEAT CRÊPES WITH
MAPLE-POACHED APPLE FILLING

Tender maple-poached apple slices and orange-laced ricotta cheese are stuffed into these nutty-tasting crêpes. Garnish the plate with juicy slices of apples or winter pears.

16	Buckwheat Crêpes (p. 100)	16
Filling:		
4	large firm apples (like Granny Smith or Northern Spy)	4
2 tbsp	unsalted butter	25 mL
1 cup	maple syrup	250 mL
1 cup	ricotta or cottage cheese	250 mL
1 to 2 tsp	grated orange rind	5 to 10 mL

Filling: Peel and slice apples thinly. In nonstick skillet, heat butter over medium heat; cook apples for 2 to 3 minutes or until warmed through. Pour in syrup; cook, uncovered, for 4 to 6 minutes or until apples are tender. With slotted spoon, remove apples and keep warm. Pour syrup into heatproof pitcher; keep warm.

Blend ricotta cheese, orange rind and 2 tbsp (25 mL) of the warm syrup; evenly divide among crêpes. Add 2 or 3 apple slices to each crêpe; roll up and place on heated serving plates. Top with remaining apple slices. Pass syrup separately. *Makes 6 to 8 servings.*

HONEY-SCENTED GRANOLA

Perhaps it's my imagination, but honey seems to be one of my basic comfort foods. Sitting downstairs on the counter is a big jar of fireweed wild-blossom honey that we carefully had transported back here to Ontario from Saltspring Island in B.C. I've had an incredible amaretto honey from Prince Edward Island and light, almost white, wild raspberry flower honey from the mountains of B.C. From the Prairies comes canola honey, which is probably the best balanced in flavor of them all. And then there's rich, caramel-colored buckwheat honey, the stuff my grandfather drizzled on buttered white bread.

Honey is like good wine, with its own particular scent, flavor and color, all of which vary from year to year. If the bees get into a stand of evergreen trees, the fireweed honey has a peculiar piney aftertaste. Enjoy your own particular vintage and for heaven's sake, save some for me!

4 cups	rolled oats, preferably old-fashioned	1 L
1 cup	hulled sunflower, sesame or pumpkin seeds	250 mL
½ cup	wheat germ	125 mL
½ cup	wheat bran	125 mL
½ cup	shredded coconut	125 mL
½ cup	chopped walnuts, pecans or almonds	125 mL
½ cup	wildflower honey	125 mL
½ cup	canola or safflower oil	125 mL
½ cup	raisins or other dried fruits	125 mL

Preheat oven to 300°F (150°C).

In large lightly greased roasting pan, toss together rolled oats, seeds, wheat germ, wheat bran, coconut and nuts. Whisk together honey and oil; pour over cereal mixture and mix well. Bake for 40 to 60 minutes or until golden, stirring frequently to prevent burning. While cooling, add raisins. Store in airtight containers or freeze. *Makes 8 cups (2 L).*

YEAST BREADS —
FROM BASIC TO BRIOCHE

BASIC WHITE BREAD

Over the years, I have become very lazy when making bread. I use a fast-acting yeast called Fermipan that I buy at our local bakery or at the health food store in Fergus, Ontario. The wildflower honey I use in this recipe gives the bread a special taste. Experiment with your own local honeys. It also helps the bread to rise more quickly than usual, even at room temperature, and gives the loaves rich golden crusts.

3 cups	very warm water	750 mL
2	large eggs	2
1 tbsp	salt	15 mL
⅓ cup	wildflower or clover honey	75 mL
6 to 7 cups	unbleached all-purpose flour	1.5 to 1.75 L
1½ tbsp	Fermipan or bakers' yeast	20 mL

In large mixing bowl, whisk together water, eggs, salt and honey. Beat in 1 cup (250 mL) of the flour. Beat in yeast. Beat in enough of the remaining flour, 1 cup (250 mL) at a time, to make soft sticky dough.

Turn dough out onto well-floured surface; knead vigorously for 5 to 7 minutes or until smooth and elastic. (The bubbles pop and squeak when kneaded sufficiently.)

Return dough to well-oiled bowl, turning to grease all over. Cover and let rise at room temperature until doubled in size, 1 to 1½ hours.

Punch dough down; divide into 3 segments. Shape into loaves and place in lightly greased 9- x 5-inch (2 L) loaf pans. Slash each loaf several times with sharp knife. Cover and let rise again at room temperature about 1 hour or until doubled and puffed.

Preheat oven to 350°F (180°C). Bake loaves for 25 to 30 minutes or until golden and hollow-sounding when tapped on bottoms, watching carefully during final minutes of baking. Let cool on wire cake racks.

Makes 3 loaves.

OLD-FASHIONED POTATO BREAD

The secret ingredient in many bread recipes is either potato-cooking water or mashed potatoes incorporated into the dough. Here's a recipe that I make when I only want two loaves.

2	potatoes, peeled and diced	2
2 cups	water	500 mL
2 tsp	salt	10 mL
2 tbsp	granulated sugar	25 mL
¼ cup	shortening	50 mL
4½ cups	unbleached all-purpose flour	1.125 L
1 tbsp	instant yeast (Fermipan is great)	15 mL

In saucepan, combine potatoes, water and salt; cover and bring to boil. Reduce heat and simmer for 15 to 20 minutes or until tender.

Drain, reserving liquid; mash thoroughly. Stir in sugar, shortening and reserved water. Transfer to large mixing bowl and let cool till lukewarm.

Beat in 1 cup (250 mL) of the flour. Beat in yeast. Beat in enough of the remaining flour to make stiff dough. Turn out onto floured surface; knead adding flour as needed to keep from sticking, for 5 to 6 minutes or until smooth and elastic.

Place in well-greased bowl, turning to grease all over. Cover and let rise in warm place for 1½ to 2 hours or until doubled.

Punch down dough. Divide in half and shape into 2 round loaves. Place on greased baking sheet; cover and let rise until doubled, about 1 hour.

Preheat oven to 400°F (200°C). Bake loaves for 30 to 35 minutes or until deep golden and hollow-sounding when tapped on bottoms. Let cool on cake racks. *Makes 2 loaves.*

CORNMEAL MOLASSES BREAD

This is a Nova Scotian recipe that keeps popping up all over Canada. It is truly great with some of our marvelous Canadian cheeses . . . Oka and Cheddar are my favorites.

1 cup	very hot milk	250 mL
1 cup	boiling water	250 mL
1 cup	yellow cornmeal	250 mL
3 tbsp	shortening or butter	50 mL
½ cup	fancy molasses	125 mL
2 tsp	salt	10 mL
2 tbsp	active dry yeast	25 mL
1 tsp	granulated sugar	5 mL
½ cup	lukewarm water	125 mL
5 to 6 cups	unbleached all-purpose flour	1.25 to 1.5 L

In large bowl, stir together hot milk, boiling water and cornmeal; stir in shortening, molasses and salt. Let cool to lukewarm.

Meanwhile, combine yeast, sugar and lukewarm water; let stand for 10 minutes or until frothy. Add to cornmeal mixture. Beat in flour, a cupful at a time, until dough is stiff. Turn out onto floured surface and knead in enough of the remaining flour so that dough has no wet spots. Continue to knead for 5 minutes or until dough is smooth and elastic.

Place dough in well-greased bowl, turning to grease all over. Cover and let rise for 1½ hours in warm place or until doubled in bulk.

Punch down dough; shape into 2 or 3 loaves. Place in greased loaf pans. Cover and let rise until doubled, about 1¼ hours.

Preheat oven to 350°F (180°C). Bake loaves for 35 to 40 minutes or until golden and hollow-sounding when tapped on bottom. Let cool on wire cake racks. *Makes 2 or 3 loaves.*

ROSEMARY-PERFUMED FLATBREAD

•••

This fragrant bread is a variation of foccacia, the Italian flatbread. I first had it in a very small cafe in Duncan, British Columbia. Drizzled with olive oil, it is great with a nourishing winter soup like Sylvia's Minestrone (p. 10) and a wedge of strong Cheddar.

If you can find fresh rosemary, use it. I have a plant that has survived my black thumb approach to gardening for three years now, and when it needs a trim, I make this bread.

1 cup	lukewarm water	250 mL
1 tsp	granulated sugar	5 mL
1 tbsp	active dry yeast	15 mL
¼ cup	olive oil	50 mL
1 tsp	salt	5 mL
2½ to 3 cups	unbleached all-purpose flour	625 to 750 mL
1 tsp	coarse salt	5 mL
2 tsp	dried rosemary, crushed	10 mL
1 or 2	garlic cloves, finely minced	1 or 2

In medium-sized mixing bowl, stir together water and sugar. Sprinkle with yeast and let stand for 10 minutes or until frothy. Add 2 tbsp (25 mL) of the olive oil and salt. Stir in 2 cups (500 mL) of the flour, a cupful at a time, until smooth. Add enough of the remaining flour to make soft dough.

Turn out dough onto lightly floured board; knead until smooth and elastic, about 5 minutes. Place dough in well-oiled bowl, turning to grease all over. Cover and let rise until doubled, about 1½ hours.

Punch down dough; roll or pat into rectangle to fit lightly greased 12- x 15-inch (30 x 38 cm) cookie sheet. With fingertips, make indentations all over dough. Sprinkle with coarse salt, remaining olive oil, rosemary and garlic.

Preheat oven to 400°F (200°C). Bake dough on bottom rack for 25 to 30 minutes or until golden brown. Let cool on wire rack or serve immediately. *Makes 1 large flatbread, or 4 to 6 servings.*

SOURDOUGH STARTER

In the days of the Klondike gold rush, this starter was the only yeast the pioneers had. The actual making of sourdough was done in the summer months when a bowl of flour and water was set outside to catch the wild yeast floating by in the air. Sometimes it worked, sometimes it didn't.

These days, we speed up the whole process by buying yeast. In both cases, the starter was the yeast basis for many baked products such as the recipes that follow. The trick is to feed it and keep it healthy by using it at least once a week.

1 tbsp	active dry yeast	15 mL
2 cups	warm water	500 mL
3 tbsp	granulated sugar	50 mL
1 tsp	salt	5 mL
2 cups	all-purpose flour	500 mL

In bowl, dissolve yeast in warm water; stir in sugar and salt. By hand, beat in flour. Transfer to empty shortening tin or any large container with lid. It needs space to grow in. Leave at room temperature for three days, stirring down each day. By this time it should have a sour smell. Use or refrigerate.

Feed the starter after use or every few days with the following:

1 cup	milk	250 mL
1 cup	all-purpose flour	250 mL
½ cup	granulated sugar	125 mL

Note: If you need to go away for several days, it can be frozen. On returning, thaw it at room temperature and feed it before putting it back into the refrigerator.

WHOLE WHEAT SOURDOUGH BREAD

Vary the bread with the addition of blackstrap instead of fancy molasses, and try some cracked wheat, sunflower or even flax seeds.

1 cup	lukewarm water	250 mL
1 tsp	granulated sugar	5 mL
1 tbsp	active dry yeast	15 mL
2 cups	Sourdough Starter (p. 108)	500 mL
2	eggs	2
⅓ cup	molasses	75 mL
1 tbsp	salt	15 mL
2 tbsp	vegetable oil	25 mL
2 cups	whole wheat flour	500 mL
3½ cups	unbleached all-purpose flour	875 mL
1 tbsp	milk	15 mL
1 tbsp	wheat germ	15 mL

In large warm bowl, stir together water and sugar. Sprinkle with yeast; let stand for 10 minutes or until frothy.

Beat in Sourdough Starter, eggs, molasses, salt and oil until combined completely. Add whole wheat flour and all-purpose flour, a cupful at a time, beating well after each addition.

Turn out dough onto floured surface; knead for 4 to 6 minutes or until smooth and very elastic. Place in well-oiled bowl, turning to grease all over. Cover and let rise in warm place until doubled, 1½ to 2 hours.

Punch down dough; divide in 2 pieces. Shape into loaves or rounds and place in greased 9- x 5-inch (2 L) loaf pan or on baking sheet. Cover and let rise again for 1½ hours or until doubled. Brush with milk and sprinkle with wheat germ.

Preheat oven to 350°F (180°C). Bake loaves for 30 minutes or until golden and hollow-sounding when tapped on bottom. Let cool on wire cake racks. *Makes 2 loaves.*

SOURDOUGH DARK RYE BREAD

This bread is great with summer sausage, some mild cheese and a bit of butter.

1 ¾ cups	warm water	425 mL
1 tsp	granulated sugar	5 mL
1 tbsp	active dry yeast	15 mL
1 cup	Sourdough Starter (p. 108)	250 mL
½ cup	molasses	125 mL
½ cup	cooked leftover 7-grain cereal (optional)	125 mL
2 tbsp	unsweetened cocoa powder, (Dutch if available)	25 mL
¼ cup	vegetable oil	50 mL
2 tsp	salt	10 mL
3 cups	unbleached all-purpose flour	750 mL
2 cups	dark rye flour	500 mL
	Rye flakes or wheat germ	

In large warm bowl, stir together ½ cup (50 mL) of the warm water, sugar and yeast. Let stand for 10 minutes or until frothy.

Stir in Sourdough Starter. Add molasses, cereal (if using), cocoa, oil, salt and all-purpose flour; beat thoroughly. Add about 1½ cups (375 mL) of the rye flour.

Sprinkle remaining rye flour on work surface. Turn out dough onto surface and knead for 4 to 6 minutes or until smooth and elastic. Place dough in well-oiled bowl, turning to grease all over. Cover and let rise in warm place for 1½ to 2 hours or until doubled. Punch down dough; shape into 2 round loaves.

Sprinkle 2 greased baking sheets with rye flakes. Place loaves on top; slash tops with sharp knife. Cover and let rise for another 1 to 1½ hours until doubled.

Preheat oven to 350°F (180°C). Bake loaves for 35 to 40 minutes or until hollow-sounding when tapped on bottom. Let cool on wire cake racks. *Makes 2 loaves.*

SOURDOUGH CINNAMON BUNS

This is one of the gooiest, yummiest cinnamon bun recipes you'll ever make. Because they are so sticky, it is essential that you use a nonstick pan or line your baking dish with parchment paper. After baking, loosen the edges and turn the buns out immediately onto the serving plate. You may wish to sprinkle chopped maraschino cherries or nuts over the caramelized surface.

⅓ cup	butter, softened	75 mL
¾ cup	lightly packed brown sugar	175 mL
1½ tsp	cinnamon	7 mL
1½ cups	unbleached all-purpose flour	375 mL
1 tbsp	granulated sugar	15 mL
2 tsp	baking powder	10 mL
½ tsp	baking soda	2 mL
1½ cups	Sourdough Starter (p. 108)	375 mL
⅓ cup	vegetable oil	75 mL
¼ cup	chopped pecans or walnuts	50 mL

Preheat oven to 400°F (200°C).

In small bowl, mix together butter, brown sugar and 1 tsp (5 mL) of the cinnamon; set aside.

Into separate bowl, sift together flour, granulated sugar, baking powder, baking soda and remaining cinnamon. Make a well in centre; pour in Sourdough Starter and oil. Mix until combined.

Turn out onto well-floured surface; knead lightly. Pat or roll into 12- x 9-inch (30 x 23 cm) rectangle. Spread with brown sugar mixture. Handling carefully, roll up from wide side. Pinch ends closed and cut into 1-inch (2.5 cm) slices.

Place, cut sides down, in nonstick or parchment paper-lined 12-inch (30 cm) pie plate or 2 smaller pans. Bake for 18 to 20 minutes or until sugar is bubbling. *Makes 12 buns.*

CHEDDAR-ONION
SOURDOUGH BISCUITS

....

G reat with homemade soup on a frosty day!

1 cup	stone ground whole-wheat flour	250 mL
1 cup	unbleached all-purpose flour	250 mL
1 tbsp	baking powder	15 mL
1 tsp	baking soda	5 mL
½ cup	vegetable oil	125 mL
2 cups	Sourdough Starter (p. 108)	500 mL
1 cup	finely diced Cheddar cheese	250 mL
½ cup	minced green onion	125 mL

Preheat oven to 400°F (200°C).

In large bowl, stir together whole wheat and all-purpose flours, baking powder, baking soda, oil, Sourdough Starter, cheese and onion. Mix until dough pulls away from side of bowl.

Turn out dough onto floured board; cut into two equal pieces. Pat each piece into 8-inch (20 cm) circle; cut into 6 or 8 pie-shaped wedges. Roll wedges up from wide end, bending a little to form crescent shape. Place on greased baking sheet. Bake for 20 minutes or until oozing cheese and golden. *Makes 12 or 16 biscuits.*

LILLIAN KAPLUN'S
SWEET YEAST DOUGH

L illian is one of Canada's most distinguished baking teachers. She began in Toronto in the 1950s and her students and their offspring have gone on to become the backbone of that city's food community. Joanne Yolles, the superstar pastry chef at Scaramouche restaurant, uses Lillian's recipes. Pearl Geneen, founder of Toronto's first cooking school and mother of Lucy Waverman, a high-profile international foodie, took Lillian's classes. Dufflet Rosenberg's mother learned some aspects of her craft from Lillian. As Joanne Kates wrote in her *Globe and Mail* column, "Mrs. Kaplun's great gift is bringing the secrets of the grandmothers to the 20th century."

These recipes came from Lillian's collection *For the Love of Cooking & Baking*.

¼ cup	lukewarm water	50 mL
1 tsp	granulated sugar	5 mL
1 tbsp	active dry yeast	15 mL
	OR	
1	fresh yeast cake	1
½ cup	soft shortening, butter or margarine	125 mL
½ cup	granulated sugar	125 mL
1 tsp	salt	5 mL
1 cup	scalded milk, cooled to almost lukewarm	250 mL
2	eggs	2
4½ cups	all-purpose flour	1.125 L

In warm bowl, combine lukewarm water and 1 tsp (5 mL) of the sugar; sprinkle in yeast; let stand for 10 minutes or until frothy.

In large mixing bowl, combine shortening, ½ cup (125 mL) sugar and salt; pour in scalded milk, stirring until sugar is dissolved. In separate bowl, beat eggs for 1 minute. Add to milk mixture, blending thoroughly. Let cool to lukewarm. Stir in yeast mixture.

With electric mixer, beat in 3 cups (750 mL) of the flour; beat for 5 minutes; beginning at low speed and gradually turning to high. Beat in remaining flour, a cupful at a time, to make soft dough. Or knead in remaining flour on floured surface until smooth and elastic, about 3 minutes. Transfer to large well-greased bowl, turning to grease all over. Cover with plastic wrap and towel. Refrigerate for 6 to 8 hours minimum until doubled, or for up to 2 days.

Before shaping into any of the following recipes, let dough stand at room temperature for 1 hour.

CINNAMON ORANGE CHELSEA BUNS

Half	Lillian Kaplun's Sweet Yeast Dough (p. 113)	Half
½ cup	packed brown sugar	125 mL
¼ cup	butter, softened	50 mL
½ tsp	cinnamon	2 mL
1 tsp	grated orange rind	5 mL
	Additional brown sugar, maraschino cherries, whole pecans, almonds or walnuts, butter	

Turn out dough onto floured board; roll out into 10- x 18-inch (25 x 45 cm) rectangle. Combine brown sugar, softened butter, cinnamon and orange rind; spread evenly over dough. Roll into long cylinder; cut into 1-inch (2.5 cm) slices.

Into 18 well-greased muffin cups, place 1 tsp (5 mL) brown sugar, a cherry, some nuts and a dab of butter. Top each with cinnamon roll sliced side up, making sure it is straight. Cover and let rise for 1½ to 2 hours or until doubled.

Preheat oven to 400°F (200°C). Bake for 12 to 15 minutes or until golden. Turn out onto serving plate while still warm. *Makes 18 buns.*

LILLIAN KAPLUN'S GOLDEN CROWN

¾ cup	granulated sugar	175 mL
1 tsp	cinnamon	5 mL
½ cup	finely chopped walnuts or pecans	125 mL
½ cup	golden raisins, chopped	125 mL
Half	Lillian Kaplun's Sweet Yeast Dough (p. 113)	Half
½ cup	melted butter	125 mL

In small bowl, toss together sugar, cinnamon, nuts and raisins; set aside.

Divide dough into small golf-ball shapes. Dip into melted butter; roll in sugar mixture. Place in even layers in well-greased 10-inch (4 L) tube pan. Sprinkle with remaining sugar mixture. Cover and let rise until doubled in bulk, 1 to 1½ hours.

Preheat oven to 375°F (190°C). Bake for 25 to 30 minutes or until puffed and richly golden. Let stand in pan for 2 to 5 minutes before loosening and inverting onto plate. *Makes 8 to 10 servings.*

ALMOND STRIPS

⅔ cup	unblanched ground almonds	150 mL
¼ cup	liquid honey	50 mL
¼ cup	butter, softened	50 mL
Half	Lillian Kaplun's Sweet Yeast Dough (p. 113)	Half
Glaze:		
¼ cup	icing sugar	50 mL
1 tbsp	milk or orange juice	15 mL

In small bowl, mix together almonds, honey and butter; set aside.

Turn out dough onto floured surface and roll out into large rectangle about 24 x 10 inches (60 x 25 cm). Spread with almond mixture. Starting at widest side, roll up into jelly roll shape; pat firmly until ½-inch (1 cm) thick and about 24 inches (60 cm) long. Slice crosswise in 1-inch (2.5 cm) strips; twist each and place 1½ inches (4 cm) apart on greased baking sheets. Cover and let rise for 45 to 60 minutes or until doubled.

Preheat oven to 375°F (190°C). Bake for 20 minutes or until golden.

Glaze: Mix together icing sugar and milk; brush over warm strips. Let cool completely. *Makes 18 to 20 strips.*

PRIZE-WINNING DINNER ROLLS

The Mount Forest Fall Fair in Ontario has been held every autumn since 1859. Like all rural Canadian fairs, it has been a showcase for the very best in community baking, pickling and preserving. These rolls were my mother's entry and won first prize in their category.

She originally designed them to be refrigerator rolls, but the standard warm rising works as well. I've included both variations.

2½ cups	warm water	625 mL
1 cup	granulated sugar	250 mL
2 tbsp	active dry yeast	25 mL
3	eggs	3
2 tsp	salt	10 mL
1 cup	vegetable oil	250 mL
8 cups	unbleached all-purpose flour	2 L
	Additional flour for kneading	

In large bowl, combine ½ cup (125 mL) of the warm water with 1 tsp (5 mL) of the sugar. Sprinkle yeast over and let stand 10 minutes or until frothy. Whisk in remaining water, sugar, eggs, salt and oil until thoroughly mixed.

Whisk in flour, a cupful at a time, beating in final amount with wooden spoon, to make soft sticky dough. Turn out onto well-floured surface. Knead for 4 to 5 minutes, dusting occasionally with flour, until dough is smooth and elastic. Place dough in well-oiled bowl, turning to grease all over.

Refrigerator Method: Cover dough with plastic wrap and heavy towel. Refrigerate for 12 hours or overnight. Punch down dough and shape into rolls. Place ½ inch (1 cm) apart on well-greased baking sheet. Let rise at room temperature for 2 hours or until well puffed and doubled.

Room Temperature Method: Cover dough with plastic wrap; let rise in warm place for 1½ to 2 hours or until doubled. Punch down dough and shape into rolls. Place ½ inch (1 cm) apart on well-greased baking sheet. Cover loosely and let rise until doubled and puffed, 1½ to 2 hours.

Both Methods: Preheat oven to 375°F (190°C). Bake rolls for 12 to 15 minutes or until hollow-sounding when tapped on bottoms.

Makes 3½ dozen.

V A R I A T I O N :

For Sesame or Poppy Seed Buns, dip the shaped dough into a cup of water or milk and then roll in seeds before placing on greased baking sheet for second rising.

LATVIAN PIRADZINI

. . . .

No special occasion could possibly be celebrated in the scattered Latvian communities of Canada without these bacon-stuffed buns. I first tasted them when I was a kid growing up.

½ lb	lean side bacon, diced	250 g
1 or 2	small onions, finely minced	1 or 2
1	green onion, minced	1
½ cup	finely diced ham (optional)	125 mL
½ tsp	pepper	2 mL
Half	dough for Prize-Winning Dinner Rolls (p. 117)	Half
1	egg yolk	1
¼ cup	milk	50 mL

In heavy saucepan, cook bacon, onions, green onion, ham (if using) and pepper over medium heat, stirring constantly, for 4 to 5 minutes or until onion is softened and bacon limp but not browned. Let cool completely.

Divide dough into 20 pieces. Roll each piece to flatten slightly. Place spoonful of bacon mixture onto centre of each. With floured fingertips, pinch edges closed to make crescents. Place about 2 inches (5 cm) apart on well-greased baking sheet; slash tops with sharp knife. Cover loosely with towel and let rise for 1½ hours or until doubled in bulk.

Preheat oven to 375°F (190°C). Whisk together egg yolk and milk; brush over crescents. Bake buns for 12 to 15 minutes or until very well browned. *Makes 20 buns.* .

TANYA'S LATVIAN-STYLE BAGELS

Tanya Barsevski, a lovely lady who cooked at my high school, says that you know you have enough flour in the dough when it puffs back at you. Homemade bagels are a treat every true bagel fan should bake at least once in a lifetime.

2 cups	warm water	500 mL
1 tbsp	granulated sugar	15 mL
2 tbsp	active dry yeast	25 mL
4	eggs, beaten	4
½ cup	vegetable oil	125 mL
1 tsp	salt	5 mL
6 to 6½ cups	all-purpose flour	1.5 to 1.625 L
Poaching Liquid:		
8 cups	boiling water	2 L
¼ cup	granulated sugar	50 mL
Glaze:		
1	egg yolk	1
¼ cup	milk	50 mL
	Poppy or sesame seeds	

In large bowl, combine 1 cup (250 mL) of the warm water with sugar. Sprinkle in yeast and let stand for 10 minutes or until frothy.

Beat in remaining water, eggs, oil and salt. Beat in flour, a cupful at a time, working final cupfuls in by hand to make soft sticky dough.

Turn out dough onto floured board; knead for 5 minutes until smooth and elastic. Place dough in well-oiled bowl, turning to grease all over. Cover and let rise until doubled, about 1½ hours.

Punch down dough and turn out onto floured board. Cut into 24 to 30 pieces. Roll each into 6-inch (15 cm) long cylinder; form into circle, twisting and pinching ends together. Place on well-greased or parchment-lined baking sheet. Cover and let rise for 15 to 20 minutes or until puffy.

Preheat oven to 450°F (230°C).

Poaching Liquid: In large saucepan, bring boiling water and sugar to boil over medium-high heat. Add bagels, 3 or 4 at a time, turning with chopsticks or wooden spoon handle, and cook for 3 minutes. Remove with slotted spoon and place on greased baking sheet.

Glaze: Whisk together egg yolk and milk; brush over bagels. Sprinkle with poppy or sesame seeds. Bake for 15 to 20 minutes or until golden browned. Store in airtight container or freeze. *Makes 2 to 2½ dozen.*

HERBED BATTER BREAD

This is the fastest yeast bread I know how to make. The texture is a bit open, but the flavor is terrific, especially when laced with lots of fresh or dried herbs. Great with soup!

1 tbsp	active dry yeast	15 mL
1 cup	lukewarm milk	250 mL
1 tsp	salt	5 mL
2	large eggs, well beaten	2
⅓ cup	butter or shortening, melted and cooled	75 mL
2 tbsp	liquid honey	25 mL
1 tbsp	minced chives or green onion	15 mL
1 tbsp	minced fresh parsley	15 mL
2 tsp	chopped dried dillweed, basil or marjoram	10 mL
3 cups	unbleached all-purpose flour	750 mL

In bowl, stir yeast into milk until dissolved. Beat in salt, eggs, melted butter, honey, chives, parsley and dillweed.

Add 2 cups (500 mL) of the flour; beat for 3 minutes by hand or 1 minute with electric mixer. Work in remaining flour to make very soft, sticky dough. Cover bowl and let rise for 1 hour or until doubled in bulk.

Stir dough down. With well-oiled hands, transfer to well-greased or nonstick 10-inch (4 L) tube pan. Cover and let rise for 30 minutes.

Place pan in COLD oven; turn heat to 350°F (180°C). Bake for 30 minutes or until golden. *Makes 1 loaf.*

PETER'S BRIOCHE

Peter Skoggard is a musician and composer but in his "former" life he operated one of Toronto's first completely vegetarian cafes. People came from across the city to consume his Sunday morning brioche. His food vocabulary is as complex and educated as is his musical talent and there is little doubt that he brings a bit of magic to the kitchen.

According to Peter, brioche goes against every bread-baking tenet in the book: too much butter, too many eggs . . . But made on a cool day according to his instructions, and with a little prayer, it will be the best, richest and most sensuous bread you will ever make.

Yeast Sponge:

½ cup	warm water	125 mL
1 tsp	liquid honey	5 mL
2 tbsp	active dry yeast	25 mL
¾ cup	unbleached all-purpose flour	175 mL

Brioche Dough:

4 cups	unbleached all-purpose flour	1 L
1 tbsp	salt	15 mL
⅓ to ½ cup	liquid honey	75 to 125 mL
8	eggs	8
1 cup	butter, softened	250 mL
	Additional flour	

Egg Wash:

1	egg yolk, well beaten	1
2 tbsp	milk	25 mL

Yeast Sponge:

Rinse small bowl in hot water to warm it. Add warm water, honey and yeast. Stir and set aside to puff, about 10 minutes. Sprinkle with flour, stirring with fork until thick batter. Let rise in warm place for 10 minutes, or until sponge-like.

Brioche Dough:

Measure flour and salt into large bowl. Make well in centre and pour in honey, using more if you prefer a sweeter bread. Add eggs and mix until sticky and well blended. Turn out onto lightly floured board; knead vigorously for 4 to 5 minutes or until smooth and satiny in texture.

Divide dough in half and flatten slightly on lightly floured surface. Scrape yeast sponge onto one half. Fold edges of dough up and around. Knead 10 to 15 times or until sponge is almost absorbed. Flatten remaining dough and place sponge/dough mixture on top. Fold edges of dough up and around. Knead for 2 to 3 minutes or until yeast is evenly distributed, adding only enough flour to keep it from sticking to work surface.

With fork, mash butter roughly; gather into ball in your hands. Knead briefly to ensure it is softened; it should be consistency of dough, not melting.

Half the dough; flatten with heel of your hand, squish butter into it. Fold it up and knead for a few turns, gathering and folding gently. Flatten remaining dough; place piece containing butter in centre and knead it in. The dough will be very sticky. Return it to mixing bowl and continue to fold and turn until butter is well blended. Turn dough onto lightly floured surface; knead for 1 minute.

Place in floured bowl; cover and let rise for 1½ to 2 hours. (This first rising takes the longest because "the yeasts are overcoming their environmental difficulties.") When doubled in bulk, punch down and let rise again until doubled, about 1 hour.

Punch down and shape. (See variation on p. 124).

For Classic Brioche, thoroughly grease 18 brioche molds (they look like deeply fluted tart tins) or large muffin tins. Divide dough into 18 pieces. To shape each brioche, tear small chunk of dough about size of a marble off piece with which you are working. Roll both into round shapes, making small tail on tiny piece. Place larger ball into prepared brioche pan. Poke finger into centre of it and imbed tail of smaller piece firmly into brioche. Repeat using all dough.

Cover and let rise again until doubled.

Preheat oven to 350°F (180°C).

Egg Wash: Stirring together beaten yolk and milk. Brush very gently over surface of brioche. Bake until richly golden, about 20 minutes. Let cool for 15 to 30 minutes before removing from pan. Complete cooling on cake rack. *Makes 18 brioche.*

BRANDIED APRICOT BRIOCHE BRAID

Drizzle with a little Orange Butter Icing (p. 190) if desired.

½ cup	slivered dried apricots	125 mL
2 tbsp	orange brandy	25 mL
2 tsp	finely grated orange rind	10 mL
¼ cup	boiling water	50 mL
Quarter	Peter's Brioche dough (p. 122)	Quarter
¼ cup	all-purpose flour	50 mL

In small bowl, combine apricots, brandy and rind. Barely cover with boiling water. Let stand while dough is rising for last time.

Dedge the prepared filling in flour. Work it into dough. Braid and place onto well-greased baking sheet. Let rise for 1½ hours or until doubled. Gently brush with Egg Wash (p. 122).

Preheat oven to 375°F (190°C). Bake brioche for 25 minutes or until golden brown. *Makes 1 loaf.*

CHALLAH (BRAIDED EGG BREAD)

This is Lillian Kaplun's classic recipe that yields three glazed and golden brown braids.

¼ cup	lukewarm water	50 mL
1 tsp	granulated sugar	5 mL
1 tbsp	active dry yeast	15 mL
	OR	
1	fresh yeast cake	1
1 cup	boiling water	250 mL
1 tbsp	granulated sugar	15 mL
2 tsp	salt	10 mL
1 tbsp	vegetable oil	15 mL
2	eggs, well beaten	2
4 cups	all-purpose flour	1 L
1	egg yolk, beaten	1
2 tbsp	milk or water	25 mL
	Sesame or poppy seeds	

In small warm bowl, blend lukewarm water and 1 tsp (5 mL) sugar. Sprinkle with yeast; let stand for 10 minutes or until foamy.

In large mixing bowl, combine boiling water, 1 tbsp (15 mL) sugar, salt and oil; beat in eggs. Let cool to lukewarm.

Add yeast mixture and 2 cups (500 mL) of the flour, beating at high speed for 5 minutes. With large spatula, mix in remaining flour to make soft sticky dough. Turn out onto floured surface; knead for 2 to 3 minutes or until smooth and elastic. Place dough in well-greased bowl, turning to grease all over. Cover with plastic wrap and refrigerate for 6 to 8 hours or let rise at room temperature to 2 to 2½ hours or until doubled.

Punch down dough; cut into 4 equal pieces. On floured surface, roll out 3 of the pieces into long rectangles; slice each piece lengthwise into 3 strips. Braid 3 of the strips to make loaf; place on well-greased baking sheet. Repeat with remaining strips to make total of 3 loaves.

Cut remaining piece of dough into 3 equal pieces. Repeat rolling, slicing lengthwise and braiding to make 3 small braids. Place each on top of loaf. Let rise in warm place for 1½ hours or until doubled.

Whisk together egg yolk and milk; brush over loaves. Sprinkle with sesame seeds. Preheat oven to 400°F (200°C). Bake for 15 minutes. Reduce heat to 350°F (180°C) and bake for 35 to 45 minutes longer or until golden and hollow-sounding when tapped on bottom. *Makes 3 loaves.*

CARDAMOM SCENTED
CHRISTMAS BREAD
• •

Every Yuletide season, I bake about five batches of this bread, freeze them and decorate them at the last minute. On Christmas Eve, we deliver them to friends and neighbors.

Once you make the bread, you'll realize how versatile it is. Shape it into loaves, braids or, by stretching and bending the braids, Christmas wreaths.

Smear them with Almond Butter Icing (p. 190) and scatter them with toasted almonds and candied fruit or maraschino cherries. I've even put thick strawberry jam into the crevices.

This recipe will make 8 braids or loaves. Freeze them as I do, or prepare only half the recipe.

6 cups	warm water	1.5 L
1⅓ cups	granulated sugar	325 mL
4 tbsp	active dry yeast	60 mL
4 tsp	salt	20 mL
4	eggs, slightly beaten	4
1 cup	canola or safflower oil	250 mL
	Grated rind of 2 oranges	
1 tbsp	ground cardamom	15 mL
4 cups	mixed fruit (candied peel, cherries, chopped candied pineapple, golden raisins or drained chopped maraschino cherries)	1 L
18 cups	unbleached all-purpose flour	4.5 L

In large warm mixing bowl, combine 2 cups (500 mL) of the warm water and 1 tbsp (15 mL) of the sugar. Sprinkle with yeast and let stand for 10 minutes or until frothy. Stir in remaining warm water and sugar, salt, eggs, oil, orange rind and cardamom.

In separate bowl, toss fruit with a little of the flour just to coat. Beat flour into liquid mixture, 2 cups (500 mL) at a time, along with fruit, beating thoroughly after each addition and working in final several cups by hand.

Turn out dough onto floured board; knead for 5 to 7 minutes or until smooth and elastic. Place in greased bowl, turning to grease all over. Cover with towel and let rise in warm place until doubled, 1½ to 2 hours. Punch down dough and divide into 8 pieces.

To shape braid: Roll each piece into rectangle about 12 inches (30 cm) long. Cut 2 lengthwise slits almost to end; braid and pinch to close. Place on greased baking sheet.

To shape wreath: Roll each piece into thin strip about 4 inches (10 cm) wide and 12 to 15 inches (30 to 40 cm) long. Cut 2 lengthwise slits almost to end; braid and wind into circle, pinching ends together. Place on greased baking sheet.

To shape into loaves: Knead each piece; shape into loaf and place in well-greased 9- x 5-inch (2.5 L) loaf pans.

Cover and let rise until doubled, about 1½ hours in warm place, 2½ hours in cool. (Because I bake them in batches, I let some rise in very warm place while others in cooler spot.)

Preheat oven to 400°F (200°C). Bake for 20 minutes or until golden brown and hollow-sounding when tapped on bottom. *Makes 8 loaves.*

Variations:

These variations are courtesy of Mr. and Mrs. Jack Klein, whose Saturday morning Raisin Bread was a tradition for years in our family.

Chop Suey Loaf

Follow the recipe for Christmas bread but omit fruit. For each piece of dough:

1	egg, beaten	1
1½ cups	candied fruit and peel or currants	375 mL
¾ cup	icing sugar	175 mL
2 tbsp	milk	25 mL
	Additional candied fruit (optional)	

Roll each piece of dough into rectangle about 10- x 12-inches (25 x 30 cm). Combine egg and fruit; spread over dough. Fold in half and with sharp knife, cut into large chunks. Place chunks in well-greased 9- x 5-inch (2 L) loaf pan. Cover and let rise until doubled, about 1½ to 2 hours. Preheat oven to 375°F (190°C). Bake for 20 to 30 minutes or until deep golden. Mix icing sugar with milk; pour over loaf while still hot. Sprinkle with candied fruit if desired. *Makes 1 loaf.*

HOT CROSS BUNS

Make half the recipe for christmas bread (p. 126), substituting this spice mixture for the cardamom. Omit mixed fruit and toss in some currants and a little candied fruit for an Easter treat.

1 tsp	ground ginger	5 mL
1 tsp	ground cloves	5 mL
1 tsp	ground nutmeg	5 mL
2 tsp	cinnamon	10 mL
2 cups	currants	500 mL
1 cup	candied mixed peel	250 mL
Egg Wash:		
1	egg yolk, well beaten	1
2 tbsp	milk	25 mL
Icing:		
½ cup	cake-and-pastry flour	125 mL
2 tbsp	shortening, softened	25 mL
2 tsp	granulated sugar	10 mL

Combine ginger, cloves, nutmeg and cinnamon; add to Christmas bread in place of cardamom. Work in currants and peel instead of mixed fruit. Cut into about 48 pieces; place on well-greased baking sheet. Cover and let rise until doubled, about 1½ to 2 hours.

Egg Wash: Combine egg yolk with milk; brush over tops.

Preheat oven to 350°F (180°C).

Icing: In bowl, beat together flour, shortening, sugar and enough cold water for piping consistency. Spoon into piping bag fitted with small plain tip. Pipe long thin lines across buns to make cross. Bake for 15 to 20 minutes or until deep golden. *Makes 4 dozen.*

KLEIN'S RAISIN BREAD

Follow recipe for christmas bread (p. 126), but omit mixed fruit. For each piece of dough, knead in:

¾ cup	sultana raisins	175 mL
¾ cup	currants	175 mL

Shape into loaf and place in greased 9- x 5-inch (2 L) loaf pan. Let rise until doubled, about 1½ to 2 hours. Preheat oven to 350°F (180°C). Bake for 25 to 35 minutes or until dark brown. *Makes 1 loaf.*

EASTER BABKA

· ·

This sweet, rich Ukrainian bread is simply delicious. I serve it with mild cheese, fresh orange marmalade and lots of coffee for Easter morning breakfast.

I've hastened the rising time by using Fermipan or bakers' yeast. Also, I've reduced the number of egg yolks from the original 10 that were to be used in addition to 5 whole eggs. I am being vague as to the number of loaves because traditionally the bread is baked in well greased coffee or shortening tins.

2½ cups	milk	625 mL
1 cup	butter	250 mL
2 tsp	salt	10 mL
¾ cup	granulated sugar	175 mL
6	eggs, lightly beaten	6
1	orange, juice and rind	1
1	lemon, juice and rind	1
1 tsp	vanilla	5 mL
7 to 8 cups	all-purpose flour	1.75 to 2 L
2 tbsp	Fermipan or bakers' yeast	25 mL
2 cups	golden raisins	500 mL
Glaze:		
1½ cups	icing sugar	375 mL
¼ cup	milk	50 mL

In heavy saucepan, heat milk and butter until butter melts. Pour into large mixing bowl; whisk in salt and sugar. Beat in eggs, orange juice and rind, lemon juice and rind, vanilla and 1 cup (250 mL) of the flour. Add yeast. Beat in raisins and enough of the remaining flour to make soft dough.

Turn out onto well-floured surface; knead until smooth and elastic, about 5 minutes. Place dough in well-greased bowl, turning to grease all over. Cover and let rise in warm place for 1 to 1½ hours, or until doubled.

Punch down dough and divide in 4. Fill each greased coffee or shortening tin one-third to one-half full with a piece of dough kneaded into ball, or shape into loaves and place in greased 9- x 5-inch (2 L) loaf pans. Cover and let rise until doubled, about 1¼ hours.

Preheat oven to 350°F (180°C). Bake for 30 minutes or until golden. Let stand for 3 to 4 minutes before removing from pans and placing on soft surface (a doubled bath towel is fine). Let cool for 30 minutes before glazing.

Glaze: Mix together icing sugar and milk; drizzle over loaves. Cool completely before slicing. *Makes about 4 loaves.*

BISCUITS, COFFEECAKES, QUICK BREADS AND QUINTESSENTIAL MUFFINS

CRISPY DINNER SCONES

M y mother has used this recipe for years. It really is the perfect biscuit with a meal.

2 cups	all-purpose flour	500 mL
1 tbsp	baking powder	15 mL
½ tsp	salt	2 mL
½ cup	shortening	125 mL
1	egg	1
	Milk	

Preheat oven to 425°F (220°C).

In large bowl, sift together flour, baking powder and salt; with pastry blender or by hand, cut or rub in shortening until crumbly.

In measuring cup, whisk egg thoroughly; add enough milk to make 1 cup (250 mL). Pour into dry ingredients, mixing well with fork until no dry spots remain.

Turn out onto well-floured surface. With floured hands, pat to about ¾- to 1-inch (2 to 2.5 cm) thickness. Cut into biscuit shapes with glass that has been dipped in flour. Gently gather up trimmings and make additional biscuits. Bake on lightly greased baking sheet for 10 to 12 minutes or until tops are beginning to turn golden.

Makes 10 to 12 biscuits.

GIRDLE SCONES

In the nearby town of Fergus, Ontario, which was founded in the early 1800s by two enterprising Scots, Adam Fergusson and James Webster, it's possible to find a few of the foods of Scotland still being prepared. The mill, in operation since the 1830s, has only recently stopped roasting its own oats.

Mrs. May Thom took me into her home and demonstrated the baking of girdle scones. The girdle is a large cast iron pan . . . we know it as a griddle. The scones turn out to be crispy and deep brown on the outside, perfect with butter and marmalade. To be sure they are cooked, May pulls one apart to check, then returns it to the pan if she decides that it looks a little damp.

3½ cups	all-purpose flour	875 mL
6 tbsp	baking powder	90 mL
1 tsp	salt	5 mL
1 tbsp	granulated sugar	15 mL
¼ cup	lard or shortening	50 mL
1	egg	1
1½ cups	milk	375 mL

Heat flat cast iron pan on low heat for 10 to 15 minutes or until hot. (To test, sprinkle with a little all-purpose flour; if it browns in 10 to 15 seconds, pan is hot enough.)

Meanwhile, into large mixing bowl, sift flour, baking powder, salt and sugar; with fingertips, rub in lard until crumbly. Whisk egg with 1 cup (250 mL) of the milk. Make a well in centre of dry ingredients; pour in liquid. With wooden spoon, stir to make soft, but not sticky dough, adding more milk as needed.

Turn out onto floured board; knead 3 or 4 times. Pat or roll to no more than ¼- to ½-inch (5 mm to 1 cm) thick. With sharp knife, cut into small triangles.

Place a few at a time on pan; cook, rotating scones occasionally, for 5 to 6 minutes or until bottoms are browned. Gently flip and cook until other side is browned. Serve hot. *Makes about 2 dozen.*

FLAN AU BLÉ D'INDE
(JOHNNY CAKE)

Although this recipe is from northern New Brunswick, it's one that could have come from central Ontario or the Prairies. When the Johnny Cake is hot from the oven, maple syrup or molasses may be poured over it. As it cools it is delicious with butter and cheese and, if it happens to become stale, it makes marvellous stuffing for roasted chicken.

¾ cup	yellow cornmeal	175 mL
1 cup	all-purpose flour	250 mL
2 tsp	baking powder	10 mL
1 tsp	baking soda	5 mL
¼ cup	granulated sugar	50 mL
2	eggs, beaten	2
½ cup	milk	125 mL
½ cup	butter, softened	125 mL

Preheat oven to 350°F (180°C).

In large mixing bowl, stir or sift together cornmeal, flour, baking powder, baking soda and sugar. Whisk together eggs, milk and butter; add to dry ingredients, stirring only until combined.

Spread in well-greased 8-inch (2 L) square cake pan. Bake for 25 to 30 minutes or until beginning to turn golden. Cut and serve right from pan. *Makes 1 loaf.*

HERBED ONION BEER BREAD

This easy batter bread has a yeasty aroma and may be baked ahead of time and rewarmed. It's delicious served warm with butter.

2¾ cups	unbleached all-purpose flour	675 mL
1 tbsp	baking powder	15 mL
1 tbsp	granulated sugar	15 mL
½ tsp	salt	2 mL
1 tsp	dry mustard	5 mL
2 tsp	dried basil	10 mL
2	green onions, minced	2
1 cup	shredded old Cheddar cheese	250 mL
1	bottle (341 mL) beer, at room temperature	1
Topping:		
1	small onion, sliced into thin rings	1
¼ cup	shredded cheese	50 mL
1 tbsp	sunflower or sesame seeds (optional)	15 mL

Preheat oven to 350°F (180°C). Grease 9- x 5-inch (2 L) loaf pan thoroughly. Set aside.

In large mixing bowl, sift or stir flour with baking powder, sugar, salt and mustard. Add basil, green onions and cheese. Pour in beer, stirring to just combine. Spread evenly in prepared pan.

Topping: Arrange onion rings all over batter; sprinkle with cheese, and seeds (if using). Bake for 50 to 55 minutes or until cake tester inserted in centre comes out clean.

Remove immediately from pan. Let cool on wire cake rack for a few minutes before serving. Serve warm. *Makes 1 loaf.*

WHOLE WHEAT
BUTTERMILK SODA BREAD

This quick recipe was developed by Holly Rowland who hosted her own television food show in Halifax for years. Serve thick warm slices with butter, cheese or even marmalade.

2 cups	whole wheat flour	500 mL
2 cups	unbleached all-purpose flour	500 mL
1 tbsp	baking powder	15 mL
1 tsp	baking soda	5 mL
2 tbsp	packed brown sugar	25 mL
¼ cup	chilled butter	50 mL
1	egg, beaten	1
1¾ cups	buttermilk	425 mL

Preheat oven to 400°F (200°C).

In large mixing bowl, combine whole wheat and all-purpose flours, baking powder, baking soda and sugar. With pastry blender or two knives, cut in butter until crumbly. Combine egg and buttermilk; add all at once to dry ingredients and mix until just combined.

Turn out onto floured surface; gently knead 8 to 10 times. Cut in two and shape into round loaves. Place on well-greased baking sheets. Slash tops with sharp knife. Bake for 35 to 40 minutes or until hollow-sounding when tapped on bottoms. *Makes 2 loaves.*

GERMAN BUNS

·······················

This biscuit recipe was pencilled into my grandmother's cook-book. It is very old and I remember that they were one of my grandfather's favorite treats. They are great for Easter morning brunch. Make them a day ahead and reheat them in foil.

2 cups	sifted all-purpose flour	500 mL
½ tsp	salt	2 mL
⅓ cup	granulated sugar	75 mL
1½ tsp	baking powder	7 mL
1 tsp	baking soda	5 mL
¼ cup	butter	50 mL
¼ cup	shortening	50 mL
1	egg	1
⅔ cup	buttermilk	150 mL
Filling:		
1	egg	1
¾ cup	packed brown sugar	175 mL
½ cup	all-purpose flour	125 mL
½ cup	sultana raisins	125 mL
	Maple syrup (optional)	

Preheat oven to 375°F (190°C).

In medium bowl, sift or stir together flour, salt, sugar, baking powder and baking soda. Cut in butter and shortening finely.

Whisk together egg and buttermilk; add to dry ingredients and stir lightly to combine.

Turn out onto floured surface; knead 5 or 6 times. Roll or pat into 8- x 12-inch (20 x 30 cm) rectangle.

Filling: Combine egg, brown sugar and flour; spread over dough. Sprinkle with raisins.

Roll dough into cylinder; cut into 12 even slices. Place on well-greased baking sheet; brush with maple syrup (if using). Bake for 20 to 25 minutes or until deep golden. *Makes 1 dozen.*

GIANT BUT BASIC MUFFINS

A s a Mom I'm always conscious of additives to our foods and, of course, the cost. I concocted these large muffins with these concerns in the back of my mind. Add raisins, chocolate chips, nuts or dried fruits to this simple recipe to create your own wholesome biggies. You might sprinkle the tops with a little cinnamon sugar before baking.

	Juice and grated rind of 1 lemon	
	Milk	
⅓ cup	vegetable oil	75 mL
⅓ cup	granulated sugar	75 mL
1	egg	1
2 cups	unbleached all-purpose flour	500 mL
1 tsp	baking soda	5 mL
1 tbsp	baking powder	15 mL
½ tsp	salt	2 mL
½ to 1 cup	chocolate chips, fresh blueberries, nuts, dried fruits or raisins (optional)	125 to 250 mL

Preheat oven to 400°F (200°C).

Pour 2 tbsp (25 mL) lemon juice into measuring cup; pour in enough milk to make 1 cup (250 mL). Let stand for 10 minutes to let sour.

In large mixing bowl, beat oil, sugar and egg until thoroughly combined; stir in lemon rind. Sift together flour, baking soda, baking powder and salt; add to creamed mixture alternately with soured milk, mixing only until no dry spots remain. Fold in chocolate chips, nuts or dried fruit.

Spoon into well-greased or paper-lined large muffin cups. Bake for 20 to 25 minutes or until tops are firm to the touch.

Makes 9 to 12 large muffins.

GIANT BRAN MUFFINS
WITH RAISINS AND APPLES

The fact that these, my favorite bran muffins, are so easy to make is a real plus. When I don't have apples, I substitute pears. Instead of raisins, I'll use nuts or sunflower seeds, or leftover cranberry sauce at Christmastime. Old bananas can be puréed into the batter. I've added everything from granola to porridge.

Use any firm cooking apple like Mutsu, Idared or Northern Spy to keep these muffins wonderfully moist for days. Peel the apples before chopping if they have been waxed for storage. Unsulphured molasses is available at most health food stores.

1 tbsp	white vinegar	15 mL
1 cup	milk	250 mL
1 cup	packed dark brown sugar	250 mL
½ cup	vegetable oil	125 mL
1	egg	1
1 tsp	vanilla	5 mL
1 cup	natural bran	250 mL
⅓ cup	wheat germ	75 mL
¼ cup	unsulphured molasses	50 mL
¾ cup	unbleached all-purpose flour	175 mL
¾ cup	whole wheat flour (preferably stoneground)	175 mL
2 tsp	baking powder	10 mL
1 tsp	baking soda	5 mL
1 cup	finely diced apple	250 mL
1 cup	sultana raisins	250 mL

Preheat oven to 400°F (200°C).

In small bowl, combine vinegar and milk. Let stand for 10 minutes to sour.

In large mixing bowl, whisk together brown sugar, oil and egg until well combined; stir in vanilla, bran, wheat germ and molasses. Stir in soured milk.

In separate bowl, combine all-purpose and whole wheat flours, baking powder and baking soda. Add apple and raisins; toss to coat fruit.

Add dry ingredients to creamed mixture, stirring only until no dry spots remain. Let stand for 5 minutes.

Spoon into well-greased or paper-lined large muffin cups, mounding tops above level of pan. Bake for 18 to 20 minutes or until tops are firm to the touch.

Let stand for 10 to 15 minutes before removing.

Run knife between muffins to separate. Bang pan sharply on the counter. Tilt it on its side and rap gently until muffins fall out.

Makes 10 to 12 large muffins.

FRESH BLUEBERRY MUFFINS

Devoted British Columbian Linda Myres swears that Richmond, B.C.'s blueberries are the "biggest and the best." My friend Jocelyn Losier in New Brunswick says almost the exact same thing about the purple gems that her cousin grows there. Then there's Jean Authier in Cap à L'Aigle, Quebec, who holds the Charlevoix berries in such esteem that he calls them *perles bleu* (blue pearls). Whatever your region, fresh blueberries really are the best to use in these delicious seasonal muffins.

2	large eggs	2
⅔ cup	granulated sugar	175 mL
½ cup	butter, melted	125 mL
2 cups	buttermilk or skim milk	500 mL
1 tsp	vanilla	5 mL
3 cups	unbleached all-purpose flour	750 mL
2 tbsp	baking powder	25 mL
¼ tsp	salt	1 mL
3 cups	fresh blueberries (preferably wild)	750 mL

Preheat oven to 400°F (200°C).

In large bowl, beat eggs, sugar and butter thoroughly; stir in buttermilk and vanilla.

In separate bowl, stir or sift together flour, baking powder and salt; beat gently into egg mixture only until no dry spots remain and batter is lumpy. Fold in blueberries.

Spoon into well-greased or paper-lined muffin cups. Bake for 20 to 25 minutes or until tops are firm to the touch. *Makes 18 to 24 large muffins.*

SCENTED CARROT-PINEAPPLE
BUTTERMILK MUFFINS
·····································

Cardamom is a most fragrant spice. It may be purchased either ground or whole, in which case it must be hulled and crushed.

¼ cup	shortening	50 mL
¼ cup	butter, softened	50 mL
1 cup	granulated sugar	250 mL
2	eggs	2
1½ cups	grated carrot	375 mL
½ cup	undrained crushed pineapple	125 mL
2½ cups	all-purpose flour	625 mL
1 tbsp	baking powder	15 mL
1 tsp	ground cardamom	5 mL
1 cup	buttermilk	250 mL

Preheat oven to 375°F (190°C).

In large mixing bowl, beat together shortening, butter, sugar and eggs until light and creamy. Stir in carrot and pineapple.

In separate bowl, combine flour, baking powder and cardamom. Add all at once to creamed mixture. Pour in buttermilk and mix only until no dry spots remain.

Heap into 9 well-greased or paper-lined large muffin cups. Bake for 20 to 25 minutes or until tops are firm to the touch. Let stand for 10 minutes before removing from pan. *Makes 9 large muffins.*

BANANA-ORANGE
WHOPPERS WITH PECANS

For the best banana flavor, pick overripe bananas that your grocer is almost giving away.

½ cup	shortening	125 mL
1 cup	granulated sugar	250 mL
2	eggs	2
2 cups	all-purpose flour	500 mL
2 tsp	baking powder	10 mL
1 tsp	baking soda	5 mL
	Grated rind and juice of 1 orange	
	Buttermilk	
1 cup	mashed ripe bananas	250 mL
¼ cup	chopped pecans or whole pine nuts	50 mL

Preheat oven to 375°F (190°C).

In large mixing bowl, beat together shortening, sugar and eggs. In separate bowl, stir together flour, baking powder, baking soda and orange rind. Squeeze orange juice into measuring cup; add enough buttermilk to make ¾ cup (175 mL).

To creamed mixture, add dry ingredients, buttermilk mixture and bananas all at once; stir only until no dry spots remain. Heap into 9 well-greased or paper-lined large muffin cups. Sprinkle with nuts. Bake for 25 to 30 minutes or until tops are firm to the touch.

Let stand for 10 minutes before cutting apart and removing from pan. *Makes 9 large muffins.*

GOLDEN PUMPKIN-APRICOT MUFFINS WITH SUGARY ALMOND TOPPING

T he rounded taste of the pumpkin is spiked by the slightly citrus
tang of slivers of dried apricot that float throughout these muffins.

¼ cup	butter, softened	50 mL
¼ cup	shortening	50 mL
1 cup	packed brown sugar	250 mL
3	eggs	3
1 tbsp	lemon juice	15 mL
1 cup	puréed cooked pumpkin	250 mL
2 cups	all-purpose flour	500 mL
1 tbsp	baking powder	15 mL
1 tsp	cinnamon	5 mL
½ tsp	grated nutmeg	2 mL
½ cup	slivered dried apricots	125 mL
½ cup	buttermilk	125 mL
Topping:		
2 tbsp	brown sugar	25 mL
2 tbsp	sliced almonds	25 mL

Preheat oven to 375°F (190°C).

In large mixing bowl, beat together butter, shortening, brown sugar
and eggs until smooth. Whisk in lemon juice and pumpkin.

In separate bowl, stir together flour, baking powder, cinnamon, nutmeg and apricots. Add to creamed mixture along with buttermilk, stirring until no dry spots remain.

Heap into 9 well-greased or paper-lined giant muffin tins.

Topping: Combine brown sugar and almonds; sprinkle evenly over
muffins. Bake for 25 minutes or until topping is deep golden and tops
of muffins are firm to the touch. Let stand for 10 minutes before
removing from pan. *Makes 9 large muffins.*

LEMONY MARMALADE MUFFINS

These are the ultimate in lemon muffins, only to be baked when you have an unabashed citrus aficionada in the house. When using lemons, always wash them thoroughly before grating.

½ cup	butter, softened	125 mL
¾ cup	granulated sugar	175 mL
2	eggs	2
	Grated rind of 1 large lemon	
½ cup	orange or lemon marmalade	125 mL
½ cup	plain yogurt	125 mL
2 cups	all-purpose flour	500 mL
2 tsp	baking powder	10 mL
1 tsp	baking soda	5 mL
¾ cup	buttermilk or sour milk	175 mL
Glaze:		
	Juice from 1 large lemon	
¼ cup	granulated sugar	50 mL

Preheat oven to 375°F (190°C).

In large mixing bowl, cream together butter and sugar. Beat in eggs until smooth and creamy. Stir in lemon rind, marmalade and yogurt.

In separate bowl, stir together flour, baking powder and baking soda; add to creamed mixture all at once. Pour in buttermilk, mixing until no dry spots remain.

Heap into 10 well-greased or paper-lined large muffin cups. Bake for 20 minutes or until tops are firm to the touch. Remove from oven and set pan on baking sheet.

Glaze: Stir together lemon juice and sugar; pour over hot muffins. Let stand for 10 minutes before cutting tops apart and removing from pan. *Makes 10 large muffins.*

PUMPKIN FRUIT LOAF

If you use canned pumpkin, this loaf can be baked all year round. Steamed or baked and mashed squash is a great replacement for the pumpkin.

¼ cup	butter or shortening	50 mL
1 cup	packed brown sugar	250 mL
2	eggs	2
¾ cup	pumpkin or squash purée	175 mL
1⅔ cups	unbleached all-purpose flour	400 mL
½ tsp	salt	2 mL
1 tbsp	baking powder	15 mL
½ tsp	allspice or grated nutmeg	2 mL
½ cup	mixed candied fruits, diced	125 mL

Preheat oven to 350°F (180°C). Grease and line 9- x 5-inch (2 L) loaf pan with waxed paper.

In large bowl, cream butter until light. Beat in sugar and eggs, one at a time, until creamy. Whisk in pumpkin.

In separate bowl, stir or sift together flour, salt, baking powder and allspice; add fruit and toss to coat. Gently stir into creamed mixture.

Spread evenly in prepared pan. Bake for 50 to 55 minutes or until golden and cake tester inserted in centre comes out clean. *Makes 1 loaf.*

WHOLE WHEAT ZUCCHINI BREAD

Zucchini is one of the most positive vegetables I've ever known. Growing it will help anyone feel like a successful gardener! Peel the zucchini only if it's large and tough.

1 cup	vegetable oil	250 mL
1½ cups	granulated sugar	375 mL
3	eggs	3
2 tsp	vanilla	10 mL
½ tsp	salt	2 mL
3 cups	grated zucchini	750 mL
1½ cups	quick-cooking rolled oats	375 mL
1½ cups	whole wheat flour	375 mL
1 tsp	baking powder	5 mL
1 tsp	baking soda	5 mL
2 tsp	cinnamon	10 mL
¾ cup	shredded coconut	175 mL
¾ cup	chopped nuts	175 mL
1 cup	raisins (optional)	250 mL

Preheat oven to 325°F (160°C).

In large bowl, beat together oil, sugar, eggs, vanilla and salt; stir in zucchini.

In separate bowl, stir together oats, flour, baking powder, baking soda, cinnamon, coconut, nuts, and raisins (if using); fold into creamed mixture, combining thoroughly.

Pour into 2 well-greased 9- x 5-inch (2 L) loaf pans. Bake for 1 hour or until tester inserted in centre comes out clean. Turn out onto rack and let cool. Store in airtight container or wrap and freeze.

Makes 2 loaves.

CASHEW-YOGURT COFFEE CAKE

Purchase fresh, fragrant vanilla beans, then plunge one of them into 4-cup (1 L) jar of granulated sugar. Let it stand for several days, then use the sugar in this recipe. Brew a fresh pot of coffee or tea and enjoy!

½ cup	shortening	125 mL
1¼ cups	vanilla granulated sugar	300 mL
2	eggs	2
2 cups	unbleached all-purpose flour	500 mL
1 tsp	baking soda	5 mL
1 tsp	baking powder	5 mL
1 cup	plain yogurt	250 mL
1 tsp	cinnamon	5 mL
½ cup	chopped cashews	125 mL

Preheat oven to 350°F (180°C).

In large mixing bowl, cream together shortening and 1 cup (250 mL) of the sugar until light and fluffy. Beat in eggs. Combine flour, baking soda and baking powder; add to flour mixture alternately with yogurt. Stir together remaining sugar, cinnamon and cashews.

Spread half of the batter evenly in well-greased tube or Bundt pan; sprinkle with half of the nut mixture. Spread with remaining batter; sprinkle with remaining nut mixture. Bake for 40 to 45 minutes or until golden brown and tester inserted in centre comes out clean.

Makes 8 to 10 servings.

FRUITS-OF-SUMMER COFFEE CAKE

This is one of our favorite coffee cakes. I alter the fruit with the season — pitted sweet cherries are spectacular, as are chopped pears, apricots, peaches (as long as they aren't too juicy), raspberries or apples. I guarantee that it will bring rave reviews.

1½ cups	unbleached all-purpose flour	375 mL
½ cup	whole wheat flour	125 mL
1 cup	granulated sugar	250 mL
½ tsp	cinnamon	2 mL
½ tsp	salt	2 mL
½ tsp	baking soda	2 mL
2 cups	Sourdough Starter (p. 108)	500 mL
1 tsp	vanilla or almond extract	5 mL
2	eggs	2
⅔ cup	vegetable oil	150 mL
2 cups	prepared fruit	500 mL
	(pit the cherries, chop other fruits into ½ -inch (1 cm) pieces)	
Topping:		
1 cup	packed brown sugar	250 mL
¼ cup	butter, softened	50 mL
2 tbsp	all-purpose flour	25 mL
1 tsp	cinnamon or grated nutmeg	5 mL
½ cup	slivered almonds or pecans	125 mL

Preheat oven to 350°F (180°C).

In large bowl, sift all-purpose and whole wheat flours, sugar, cinnamon, salt and baking soda. In separate bowl, stir together Sourdough Starter, vanilla or almond extract, eggs and oil; stir into dry ingredients. Fold in prepared fruit. Spread in well-greased 9- x 13-inch (3.5 L) baking dish.

Topping: In bowl, cream together sugar and butter; stir in flour and cinnamon. Sprinkle over batter. Scatter nuts over top. Bake for 35 to 40 minutes or until tester inserted in centre comes out clean. Serve warm. *Makes 1 cake.*

DANISH PASTRY

··

This quick and easy recipe comes from my friend and walking companion Joan Rigby.

Vary the topping as you desire. I've used 2 to 3 cups (500 to 750 mL) of any sort of thickened filling I come up with — apple, cherry or blueberry (raisin doesn't work too well). Sometimes I scatter ⅓ cup (75 mL) sliced almonds over the batter before baking.

½ cup	butter, softened	125 mL
½ cup	shortening	125 mL
1 cup	granulated sugar	250 mL
1 tsp	almond extract	5 mL
1 tsp	vanilla	5 mL
4	eggs	4
3 cups	unbleached all-purpose flour	750 mL
1½ tsp	baking powder	7 mL
½ cup	milk	125 mL
2 to 3 cups	thickened pie filling	500 to 750 mL
Glaze:		
½ cup	icing sugar	125 mL
2 tbsp	milk	25 mL

Preheat oven to 350°F (180°C).

In large bowl, cream together butter and shortening; beat in sugar, almond extract, vanilla and eggs. Combine flour with baking powder; beat into creamed mixture along with milk.

Grease and flour 10- x 15-inch (25 x 38 cm) baking sheet with sides. Pour in two-thirds of batter and spread evenly. Spoon on pie filling. Drop remaining batter, by spoonfuls, over filling. Bake for 20 to 30 minutes or until richly golden.

Glaze: Mix icing sugar with milk; drizzle over warm pastry. Let cool before serving. *Makes 10 servings.*

PANFULS OF COOKIES
AND GOOEY SQUARES

WAYNE'S PEANUT BUTTER COOKIES

My husband Wayne makes the best peanut butter cookies I've ever tasted. This is his special recipe.

½ cup	shortening	125 mL
½ cup	creamy peanut butter	125 mL
½ cup	granulated sugar	125 mL
½ cup	packed brown sugar	125 mL
1	egg	1
½ tsp	vanilla	2 mL
1¼ cups	all-purpose flour	300 mL
1 tsp	baking soda	5 mL
½ tsp	salt	2 mL

Preheat oven to 375°F (190°C).

In mixing bowl, cream together shortening, peanut butter, white and brown sugars; beat in egg and vanilla.

Stir together flour, baking soda and salt; add to peanut butter mixture, blending well.

Roll into small balls; place on greased baking sheets about 1 inch (2.5 cm) apart. Press cookies lightly with floured fork to mark attractively. Bake for 10 to 12 minutes or until golden. Let cool. *Makes about 3 dozen.*

THE VERY BEST
SUGAR COOKIE RECIPE
····································

These are not only faster than the rolled variety, they taste
amazing.

1 cup	soft butter or margarine	250 mL
1 cup	vegetable oil	250 mL
1 cup	icing sugar	250 mL
1 cup	granulated sugar	250 mL
2	eggs	2
1 tsp	vanilla	5 mL
3 cups	all-purpose flour	750 mL
1¼ cups	cake-and-pastry flour	300 mL
1 tsp	baking soda	5 mL
1 tsp	cream of tartar	5 mL
½ tsp	salt	2 mL
	Granulated sugar	

Preheat oven to 350°F (180°C).

In large mixing bowl, cream together butter, oil, icing sugar and
granulated sugar until fluffy; beat in eggs, one at a time, and vanilla.

Sift or stir together all-purpose and cake-and-pastry flours, baking
soda, cream of tartar and salt; add to creamed mixture, combining
thoroughly.

Roll 1 tsp (5 mL) of the dough in granulated sugar. Place on
ungreased baking sheet about 1 inch (2.5 cm) apart; flatten with drinking glass. Bake for 10 to 12 minutes or until lightly golden.

Makes 8 to 9 dozen.

NANNA'S COCONUT CRISPS

My mother-in-law's cookie jar is almost always full — unless her grandchildren have recently raided it.

This is a very dry mixture. Use your hands to put the cookies onto the baking sheets.

1 cup	shortening	250 mL
½ cup	granulated sugar	125 mL
1 cup	packed brown sugar	250 mL
1	egg, beaten	1
1½ cups	rolled oats	375 mL
1¼ cups	sifted all-purpose flour	300 mL
1 tsp	baking powder	5 mL
1 cup	desiccated coconut	250 mL
¼ to ½ tsp	grated nutmeg	1 to 2 mL

Preheat oven to 350°F (180°C).

In medium-sized mixing bowl, cream together shortening and sugars until fluffy; beat in egg. Stir together oats, flour, baking powder, coconut and nutmeg; work into creamed mixture thoroughly.

Drop by spoonfuls about 1 inch (2.5 cm) apart onto greased baking sheets; press with fork that has been dipped in water. Bake for 8 to 12 minutes or until golden. Remove to wire cake racks and let cool.

Makes 3 to 4 dozen.

BLACK WALNUT BUTTER COOKIES

We are lucky enough to have three black walnut trees in our backyard. Each fall, we collect heaping buckets of the resinous-smelling nuts. As my sons and I hull the nuts, our hands turn yellow from the dye that seeps out of the shell.

You may see a rare basket of hulled nuts tucked away under a table or behind a vendor's stand at a farm market. Buy them and enjoy a unique fall treat.

These melt-in-your-mouth shortbread cookies are a perfect pre-Christmas treat. Use a glass with a design on the bottom to create miniature stars.

½ cup	butter, at room temperature	125 mL
½ cup	shortening	125 mL
6 tbsp	icing sugar	90 mL
1 cup	finely chopped walnuts	250 mL
2 cups	unbleached all-purpose flour	500 mL
	Granulated sugar	
	Additional icing sugar	

Preheat oven to 350°F (180°C).

In bowl, cream together butter, shortening and icing sugar; beat in walnuts and flour, mixing thoroughly.

Form into 1-inch (2.5 cm) balls; place about 1 inch (2.5 cm) apart on lightly greased baking sheet. Gently flatten each cookie with glass that has been dipped in water; then in granulated sugar. Bake for 8 to 10 minutes or until just barely golden at edges. Remove to wire cake rack; sprinkle with icing sugar while still warm. Let cool completely.

Makes 3 to 4 dozen.

VERA'S BUTTER PECAN COOKIES

These are great Christmastime cookies. Poke pecans into half the batch and slivers of maraschino cherries into the other half.

1 cup	butter or margarine	250 mL
⅔ cup	packed brown sugar	150 mL
1	egg yolk	1
2 cups	all-purpose flour	500 mL
	Pecan halves or maraschino slivers	

Preheat oven to 350°F (180°C).

In bowl, cream together butter and sugar until light and fluffy; beat in egg yolk. Stir in flour, mixing thoroughly. Gather into ball and chill for 30 to 60 minutes.

Break off chunks of dough and roll into 1-inch (2.5 cm) balls. Place on ungreased baking sheets about 2 inches (5 cm) apart. Press with floured fork to flatten slightly. Top with pecan or cherry.

Bake for 15 to 20 minutes or until barely tinged golden around edges. Remove to wire cake racks and let cool. *Makes about 4 dozen.*

LENA'S GUMDROP COOKIES

L ena Nafziger is a cookie baker par excellence . . . she makes these by the pailful and freezes them before Christmas.

1 cup	butter, softened	250 mL
1 cup	packed brown sugar	250 mL
1 cup	granulated sugar	250 mL
2	eggs, beaten	2
1 tsp	vanilla	5 mL
2 cups	all-purpose flour	500 mL
1 tsp	baking soda	5 mL
1 tsp	baking powder	5 mL
¼ tsp	salt	1 mL
1 cup	shredded coconut	250 mL
1 cup	finely diced gumdrop candies	250 mL
2 cups	rolled oats	500 mL

Preheat oven to 350°F (180°C).

In bowl, cream together butter, brown sugar and granulated sugar until light and fluffy; beat in eggs and vanilla.

Stir together flour, baking soda, baking powder and salt; add to creamed mixture along with coconut, gumdrops and rolled oats.

Drop by teaspoonfuls (5 mL) about 1 inch (2.5 cm) apart onto greased baking sheets. Press with fork that has been dipped in milk to flatten slightly. Bake for 10 to 12 minutes or until golden and firm to the touch. *Makes 4 to 5 dozen.*

ELEANOR'S MINCEMEAT COOKIES

Cookie exchanges are one of the best ways to obtain a huge selection of great treats for Christmas.

My friend Eleanor Morris uses up small bits of Christmas mincemeat in these delicious cookies.

1 cup	shortening	250 mL
2 cups	packed brown sugar	500 mL·
2	eggs	2
½ cup	water	125 mL
1 tsp	vanilla	5 mL
3½ cups	unbleached all-purpose flour	875 mL
¼ tsp	salt	1 mL
1 tsp	baking soda	5 mL
1 tsp	cinnamon	5 mL
⅔ cup	mincemeat	150 mL

Preheat oven to 400°F (200°C).

In bowl, cream together shortening and brown sugar until light and fluffy; beat in eggs. Beat in water and vanilla. Stir together flour, salt, baking soda and cinnamon; add to creamed mixture, combining thoroughly.

Drop by 1 tsp (5 mL) spoonfuls about 2 inches (5 cm) apart onto ungreased baking sheets. Place small spoonful mincemeat on top of each; cover with about ½ tsp (2 mL) of the remaining dough. Bake for 10 to 12 minutes or until golden. *Makes 3 to 4 dozen.*

KILLER MONSTER COOKIES

Named by my friend Maureen after trying to eat a whole cookie, this gi-normous recipe is really for the kids in your neighborhood — or even your town. It can be easily halved, but the cookies freeze so well that you might just like to get the mess over with once and for all.

6	eggs	6
2 cups	packed brown sugar	500 mL
2 cups	granulated sugar	500 mL
1 tbsp	vanilla	15 mL
1 tbsp	corn syrup	15 mL
4 tsp	baking soda	20 mL
1 cup	butter or margarine, softened	250 mL
2⅔ cups	peanut butter, at room temperature (about 1½ lb/750 g)	650 mL
9 cups	quick-cooking rolled oats	2.25 L
½ lb	M & M's or Smarties candies	250 g
½ lb	chocolate chips	250 g

Preheat oven to 350°F (180°C).

In very large mixing bowl, beat eggs until foamy; beat in brown and granulated sugars, vanilla and corn syrup. Add baking soda. Beat in butter and peanut butter, blending until thoroughly combined. Stir in oats, candies and chocolate chips.

Shape dough into small hamburger-sized patties. Place about 2 inches (5 cm) apart on greased baking sheets. Bake for 12 to 15 minutes or until golden brown. Let stand for a few minutes before removing from pan. *Makes 3 to 5 dozen.*

CHRISTMAS FRUIT COOKIES

I have to keep these in the freezer or they'll get eaten immediately. In fact, my husband has been known to even raid the freezer late at night when he knows no one will catch him. Make small cookies for your Christmas cookie platter and larger 2-inch (5 cm) ones for the kids to enjoy any time.

½ cup	shortening	125 mL
½ cup	butter, softened	125 mL
2 cups	granulated sugar	500 mL
3	eggs	3
1 tsp	lemon extract	5 mL
1½ tsp	vanilla	7 mL
3¼ cups	cake-and-pastry flour, sifted	800 mL
1 tsp	baking soda	5 mL
½ tsp	salt	2 mL
½ tsp	cinnamon	2 mL
½ tsp	grated nutmeg	2 mL
½ tsp	ground cloves	2 mL
½ lb	chopped dates	250 g
½ lb	chopped raisins	250 g
¼ lb	chopped candied cherries, red and green	125 g
¼ lb	candied pineapple, chopped	125 g
¼ lb	candied citrus peel	125 g
¼ cup	milk	50 mL

Preheat oven to 350°F (180°C).

In large bowl, cream together shortening, butter and sugar until light and fluffy; beat in eggs, one at a time. Beat in lemon and vanilla extracts.

In separate large bowl, stir or sift together flour, baking soda, salt, cinnamon, nutmeg and cloves. In another bowl, combine dates, raisins, cherries, pineapple and peel; add ½ cup (125 mL) of the flour mixture and toss to coat fruit. Stir flour mixture alternately with milk into creamed mixture. Fold in fruits thoroughly.

Drop by small spoonfuls about 1½ inches (4 cm) apart onto greased or parchment paper-lined baking sheets. Bake for 15 to 17 minutes or until browning around edges and golden in centers.

Makes about 12 dozen small cookies or 6 to 8 dozen 2-inch (5 cm) cookies.

WHOOPIE PIES

· ·

Here are two versions of these traditional Mennonite cookies: the first, my boys' favorite, a dark chocolate variety; the second, my favorite, a spicy pumpkin cookie. The icing is the same for both.

CHOCOLATE WHOOPIE PIES

· ·

1 cup	buttermilk	250 mL
1 tsp	white vinegar	5 mL
1 cup	shortening	250 mL
2 cups	granulated sugar	500 mL
2	eggs	2
2 tsp	vanilla	10 mL
5 cups	all-purpose flour	1.25 L
¾ cup	unsweetened cocoa powder	175 mL
1 tsp	salt	5 mL
1 cup	very hot water	250 mL
2 tsp	baking soda	10 mL
	Whoopie Pie Icing (p. 163)	

Preheat oven to 375°F (190°C).

Stir together buttermilk and vinegar; set aside for 10 minutes to let sour.

In large mixing bowl, cream together shortening and sugar thoroughly. Beat in eggs and vanilla. Sift together flour, cocoa and salt; blend into creamed mixture alternately with soured buttermilk.

In 2-cup (500 mL) measure, combine hot water with baking soda; beat into batter until completely blended.

Drop batter by heaping tablespoonfuls (15 mL) about 2 inches (5 cm) apart onto greased baking sheets. Bake for 12 to 14 minutes or until tops spring back when touched gently. Remove to wire cake racks and let cool. Sandwich with Whoopie Pie Icing. *Makes 2 dozen.*

WHOOPIE PIE ICING

½ cup	Crisco	125 mL
¼ cup	butter, softened	50 mL
5 cups	icing sugar	1.25 mL
2	egg whites	2
1 tbsp	vanilla	15 mL

In deep mixing bowl, cream together Crisco and butter: beat in icing sugar and egg whites until fluffy. Beat in vanilla. If not using immediately, cover with plastic wrap to prevent hardening.

Makes enough filling for 2 dozen Whoopie Pies.

SPICY PUMPKIN WHOOPIE PIES

1 cup	vegetable oil	250 mL
2 cups	packed brown sugar	500 mL
1½ cups	cooked pumpkin purée	375 mL
2	eggs	2
1 tsp	vanilla	5 mL
3 cups	all-purpose flour	750 mL
½ tsp	salt	2 mL
1 tsp	baking powder	5 mL
1 tsp	baking soda	5 mL
4 tsp	cinnamon	20 mL
1 tsp	ginger	5 mL
½ tsp	ground cloves	2 mL
Half	Whoopie Pie Icing (p. 163)	Half

Preheat oven to 350°F (180°C).

In large mixing bowl, beat together oil and sugar; beat in pumpkin purée. Beat in eggs, one at a time, and vanilla.

In separate bowl, sift together flour, salt, baking powder, baking soda, cinnamon, ginger and cloves; stir into pumpkin mixture to combine thoroughly.

Drop by heaping tablespoonfuls (15 mL) about 2 inches (5 cm) apart onto greased baking sheets. Bake for 12 to 15 minutes or until golden and tops spring back when touched gently. Remove to wire cake racks and let cool. Sandwich with Whoopie Pie Icing.

Makes 1 dozen.

AUTHENTIC SHORTBREAD

The best shortbread you can make!

⅔ cup	rice flour	150 mL
4 cups	all-purpose flour	1 L
1 cup	granulated sugar	250 mL
2 cups	unsalted butter, slightly softened	500 mL

Preheat oven to 275°F (140°C).

In large mixing bowl, stir together rice flour, all-purpose flour and sugar. With fork, coarsely cut in butter. Knead dough gently until smooth and soft.

Divide into three portions. Pat each into ½-inch (1 cm) thick round on ungreased baking sheets. Prick with tines of fork. Bake for 1½ hours or until golden. *Makes 3 rounds.*

MOM'S CHRISTMAS FRUIT BARS

Much like a hermit cookie, these bars are just a little faster to make.

½ cup	butter or shortening, softened	125 mL
½ cup	granulated sugar	125 mL
1	egg	1
1 tsp	grated orange rind	5 mL
2 tbsp	frozen orange juice concentrate, thawed	25 mL
¼ tsp	almond extract	1 mL
1¼ cups	unbleached all-purpose flour	300 mL
½ tsp	baking soda	2 mL
¼ tsp	salt	1 mL
⅔ cup	chopped mixed candied fruits	150 mL
½ cup	chopped pecans	125 mL
	Orange Glaze (p. 167)	

Preheat oven to 350°F (180°C).

In medium mixing bowl, cream together butter and sugar until fluffy. Beat in egg. Beat in orange rind, orange juice concentrate and almond extract.

In separate bowl, stir or sift together flour, baking soda and salt. Add fruit and nuts; toss to coat. Stir into creamed mixture until no dry spots remain.

Spread evenly in well-greased 9-inch (2.5 L) square cake pan. Bake for 15 to 20 minutes or until golden on top and tester inserted into centre comes out clean. Let cool and frost thinly with Orange Glaze. Cut into bars. *Makes about 3 dozen.*

ORANGE GLAZE

· ·

2 tbsp	butter, softened	25 mL
2 cups	icing sugar	500 mL
1 tbsp	frozen orange juice concentrate, thawed	15 mL
	Water	

In bowl, beat together butter and icing sugar; beat in orange juice concentrate and enough water to create good spreading consistency.

Makes about 1 cup (250 mL).

MOM'S DATE SQUARES

These crumbly squares are thick with citrus-scented filling . . . how could anyone resist? Not only that, they're good for you.

Filling:

2 cups	chopped pitted dates	500 mL
½ cup	granulated sugar	125 mL
1 cup	water	250 mL
	Juice and rind of 1 orange	

Crust:

⅔ cup	all-purpose flour	150 mL
⅔ cup	whole wheat flour	150 mL
½ tsp	baking soda	2 mL
1¼ cups	rolled oats	425 mL
¾ cup	butter or margarine	175 mL
1 cup	packed brown sugar	250 mL

Filling: In heavy saucepan, combine dates, sugar, water, orange juice and rind; cover and bring to boil. Reduce heat and simmer, stirring frequently, until dates are tender and liquid is absorbed, 15 to 20 minutes. Let cool.

Crust: Preheat oven to 375°F (190°C).

Stir together flours, soda and rolled oats. In bowl, cream together butter and sugar; mix in flour mixture until crumbly and moist. Pat about two-thirds of the mixture into lightly greased 9-inch (2.5 L) square cake pan. Spread filling evenly over base. Sprinkle with remaining flour mixture and pat in lightly. Bake for 25 to 30 minutes or until edges begin to turn golden. Let cool slightly before cutting.

Makes about 2 dozen.

AUNTIE VERA'S
DELICIOUS BROWNIES
•••

Few people have taught me the art of surviving a large family better than my friend Vera. This is one of her most tried and true recipes!

1 cup	butter or margarine	250 mL
4	squares unsweetened chocolate	4
2 cups	granulated sugar	500 mL
4	eggs	4
2 tsp	vanilla	10 mL
1½ cups	all-purpose flour	375 mL
½ tsp	salt	2 mL
1½ cups	chopped walnuts or pecans	375 mL
	Brownie Icing (recipe follows)	

Preheat oven to 350°F (180°C).

In small heavy saucepan over very low heat or in microwaveable dish, melt butter with chocolate. Let cool.

In large mixing bowl, beat chocolate mixture into sugar. Beat in eggs, one at a time, until lighter in color. Beat in vanilla. Stir in flour and salt until no dry spots remain. Stir in nuts.

Pour into well-greased 9- x 13-inch (3.5 L) cake pan. Bake for 25 to 30 minutes or until just set. Do not overbake. Let cool for 30 minutes before icing with Brownie Icing. Cut into squares. *Makes 3 to 4 dozen.*

BROWNIE ICING
•••••••••••••••••••••••

2	squares unsweetened chocolate	2
¼ cup	butter	50 mL
3 cups	icing sugar	750 mL
¼ to ⅓ cup	milk	50 to 75 mL
1 tsp	vanilla	5 mL

In heavy saucepan over low heat or in microwaveable dish, melt chocolate and butter. In bowl, combine icing sugar, milk and vanilla; beat in chocolate mixture until creamy.

Pour over brownies immediately or let stand for 15 minutes to thicken before spreading over brownies. *Makes about 1½ cups (375 mL).*

JEFF'S ROCKY ROAD SQUARES

Try these squares at Christmas when all caloric caution is thrown to the December winds.

	Graham wafers	
1	package (6 oz/168 g) semisweet chocolate chips	1
½ cup	butter or margarine	125 mL
1 cup	sifted icing sugar	250 mL
½ cup	chopped pecans or walnuts	125 mL
2 cups	miniature marshmallows	500 mL

Line 8-inch (2 L) square cake pan with whole graham wafers; set aside.

In heavy saucepan, melt chocolate chips and butter. Let stand for 5 minutes to cool slightly. Beat icing sugar. Fold in nuts and marshmallows. Spread over prepared base. Cover and chill before cutting into squares. *Makes 20 squares.*

MAPLE PECAN SQUARES

This is one of my father's favorite recipes. It has been handed down through generations of fine bakers.

Base:

1 cup	all-purpose flour	250 mL
¼ cup	packed brown sugar	50 mL
½ cup	butter, softened	125 mL

Topping:

⅔ cup	packed brown sugar	150 mL
1 cup	dark maple syrup	250 mL
2	eggs, beaten	2
½ tsp	vanilla	2 mL
2 tbsp	all-purpose flour	25 mL
1 cup	pecan halves	250 mL

Preheat oven to 350°F (180 °C).

Base: In small bowl, combine flour and sugar; rub in butter to make coarse crumbs. Pat firmly into 9-inch (2.5 L) square cake pan. Bake for 5 minutes. Remove and set aside.

Topping: Increase oven temperature to 425°F (220°C). In small saucepan, combine brown sugar and maple syrup; bring to boil. Reduce heat and simmer gently for 5 minutes. Let cool for 10 minutes.

Pour syrup mixture into medium-sized bowl; whisk in eggs, vanilla and flour until smooth. Stir in pecans. Pour over base. Bake for 10 minutes. Reduce heat to 350°F (180°C) and continue to bake until firm, about 15 minutes. *Makes 2 to 3 dozen.*

PEANUT BUTTER SQUARES

Our boys have been "testing" this recipe ever since they were old enough to raid Grandma's always-accessible pantry.

Base:

½ cup	butter	125 mL
¾ cup	granulated sugar	175 mL
2	eggs	2
3 cups	miniature marshmallows	750 mL
1½ cups	graham wafer crumbs	375 mL
1 tbsp	vanilla	15 mL

Topping:

2 tbsp	butter, softened	25 mL
2 tbsp	peanut butter	25 mL
1½ cups	icing sugar	375 mL
	Boiling water	

Base: In heavy saucepan, combine butter and sugar. Place over medium heat and vigorously whisk in eggs. Cook, stirring constantly, until bubbling, 5 to 7 minutes. Remove from heat and let cool to room temperature. Beat in marshmallows, crumbs and vanilla. Press into buttered 9-inch (2.5 L) square cake pan.

Topping: In bowl, cream together butter, peanut butter and icing sugar. Beat in just enough boiling water to make mixture smooth and creamy. Spread evenly over base. Cover and chill until thoroughly set.

Dip sharp knife in water before cutting into squares. Store, tightly covered, in refrigerator. *Makes 24 to 30 squares.*

CLASSIC CAKES

ANGEL FOOD CAKE

For years, this recipe was printed on the back of the Swan's Down Flour cake box. It takes almost a dozen eggs and, since we had chickens, my mother baked it whenever a special occasion arose. When serving it, she'd put a tiny juice glass of water in the centre into which she plunged a bouquet of cut flowers.

If you have never made a real angel food cake before, you owe it to yourself to try it just once. Follow the instructions carefully and let it cool completely before removing it from the tube pan. Serve as is with fresh fruit or split and frost with lightly sweetened whipped cream and fresh berries.

1 cup	sifted Swan's Down Cake flour	250 mL
1½ cups	granulated sugar	375 mL
¼ tsp	salt	1 mL
1¼ cups	egg whites, at room temperature (8 to 10 large eggs)	300 mL
1¼ tsp	cream of tartar	7 mL
1 tsp	vanilla	5 mL
¼ tsp	almond extract	1 mL

Preheat oven to 375°F (190°C).

Sift together flour, ½ cup (125 mL) of the sugar and salt four times. Set aside.

In very large bowl, beat egg whites until foamy. Sprinkle with cream of tartar; beat until soft peaks form. Beat in vanilla and almond extract. Sprinkle with remaining sugar, ¼ cup (50 mL) at a time, beating well after each addition.

Gently fold flour mixture into egg whites, a quarter at a time, blending well after each addition. Fold 14 to 20 more times.

Spread evenly and gently in 10-inch (4 L) ungreased tube pan. Bake for 35 to 40 minutes or until tester inserted in deepest part comes out clean. Invert pan onto upside down drinking glass; let cool completely. Carefully loosen edges and transfer cake to plate. Cover well before freezing or store in cake saver for up to 3 days. *Makes 10 to 12 servings.*

CLASSIC LEMON CHIFFON CAKE

Lillian Kaplun commented to me that baking, unlike cooking, is a building process, one that should be approached in a positive and patient frame of mind. Use only top-quality ingredients and never take shortcuts. Serve this cake with fresh fruit and whipped cream or simply frost it lightly and slice with a serrated knife.

2¼ cups	sifted cake-and-pastry flour	550 mL
1 tbsp	baking powder	15 mL
1⅓ cups	granulated sugar	325 mL
¾ tsp	salt	4 mL
3	egg yolks	3
⅓ cup	sunflower oil	75 mL
¾ cup	water	175 mL
2 tsp	lemon juice	10 mL
2 tsp	vanilla	10 mL
	Grated rind of 1 lemon	
1 cup	egg whites, at room temperature (about 7 eggs)	250 mL
½ tsp	cream of tartar	2 mL

Preheat oven to 325°F (160°C).

Into large mixing bowl, sift together flour, baking powder, 1 cup (250 mL) of the sugar and salt; make a well in centre. Add egg yolks, oil, water, lemon juice, vanilla and lemon rind; whisk until combined.

In large bowl, beat egg whites until foamy. Beat in cream of tartar. Gradually beat in remaining ⅓ cup (75 mL) sugar, a spoonful at a time, beating until stiff peaks form.

With same beaters, beat egg yolk mixture for 1 minute; fold into egg whites carefully, blending well.

Pour into ungreased 10-inch (4 L) tube pan, spreading evenly. Run knife through batter to release any large air bubbles.

Bake for 55 minutes. Increase heat to 350°F (180°C); bake for 15 minutes longer. Invert pan onto upside down drinking glass; let cool completely, about 1 hour. Carefully loosen edges and remove to plate. Store in tightly covered cake saver. *Makes 10 to 12 servings.*

MOM'S DATE-FILLED CHOCOLATE
CAKE WITH FUDGE ICING

No other cake meant "birthday" the way this one did. Of course, it HAD to be filled with cooked dates. It's my favorite cake! Decorate with chocolate sprinkles or chopped pecans or toasted coconut or drizzle with melted white chocolate.

½ cup	butter, softened	125 mL
2 cups	lightly packed brown sugar	500 mL
3	eggs	3
2 tsp	vanilla	10 mL
3	squares unsweetened chocolate, melted and cooled	3
2¼ cups	sifted cake-and-pastry flour	550 mL
2 tsp	baking soda	10 mL
½ tsp	salt	2 mL
1 cup	plain yogurt or sour cream	250 mL
1 cup	boiling water	250 mL
1½ cups	Date Filling (p. 177)	375 mL
	Chocolate Fudge Icing (p. 177)	

Preheat oven to 350°F (180°C). Grease and flour three 9-inch (1.5 L) round cake pans or line with parchment paper. Set aside.

In large mixing bowl, cream butter thoroughly; gradually beat in sugar. Beat in eggs, one at a time, until light and fluffy. Mix in vanilla and cooled chocolate.

Sift together flour, baking soda and salt. Stir into creamed mixture alternately with yogurt. Add boiling water, stirring to combine well and make thin batter. Pour into prepared cake pans.

Bake for 25 minutes or until tester inserted in centre comes out clean. Let stand in pans for 5 to 10 minutes before removing to wire cake racks to let cool completely.

Place bottom layer on cake plate; spread with half of the Date Filling. Place second layer on top. Spread with remaining filling. Place remaining layer on top and frost top and sides with Chocolate Fudge Icing.

Makes 12 generous servings.

DATE FILLING

· · · · · · · · · · · · · · · · · · · ·

2 cups	chopped, pitted dates	500 mL
½ cup	granulated sugar	125 mL
1 cup	water	250 mL
	Juice and rind of 1 orange	

In a heavy saucepan, combine dates, sugar, water, orange juice and rind; cover and bring to a boil. Reduce heat and simmer, stirring frequently, until dates are tender and liquid absorbed, about 15 to 20 minutes. Let cool. *Makes 2 cups (500 mL).*

CHOCOLATE FUDGE ICING

· ·

4	squares unsweetened chocolate, melted and cooled	4
½ cup	butter, softened	125 mL
3 cups	icing sugar	750 mL
¼ cup	warm milk	50 mL
1 tsp	vanilla	5 mL

In bowl, beat together chocolate and butter until smooth and creamy. Beat in icing sugar. Beat in warm milk and vanilla until of spreading consistency. *Makes about 1½ cups (375 mL).*

MOM'S BANANA CAKE

This moist and delicious cake is one of the very best, especially with Maple Cream Icing, which gets fluffier the longer you beat it. Garnish with nuts or even chocolate shot, if desired.

¼ cup	butter, softened	50 mL
1 cup	granulated sugar	250 mL
2	eggs	2
1 tsp	vanilla	5 mL
1 cup	mashed bananas	250 mL
1½ cups	sifted cake-and-pastry flour	375 mL
1 tsp	baking soda	5 mL
1 tsp	baking powder	5 mL
	Maple Cream Icing (recipe follows)	

Preheat oven to 375°F (190°C). Grease and flour two 8-inch (1.2 L) round cake pans or line with parchment paper. Set aside.

In bowl, cream together butter and sugar until light in color. Beat in eggs, one at a time, beating well after each addition. Add vanilla and bananas.

Sift together flour, baking soda and baking powder. Stir into banana mixture, mixing until no dry spots remain. Spread evenly in prepared pans.

Bake 25 to 30 minutes or until deep brown. Let stand in pans for 5 minutes before removing to wire cake racks to let cool completely.

Place bottom layer on cake plate; spread with one-quarter of the Maple Cream Icing. Place second layer on top; frost top and sides.

Makes 10 to 12 servings.

MAPLE CREAM ICING

½ cup	butter, softened	125 mL
4 cups	icing sugar	1 L
1 tsp	maple extract	5 mL
	Milk or cream	

In mixing bowl, cream butter. Beat in icing sugar, maple extract and enough milk to make fluffy spreadable consistency. *Makes 2 cups (500 mL).*

TOASTED HAZELNUT TORTE

T his flourless torte is a classic recipe that's filled with sweetened whipped cream and ripe fruit. The delicate layers freeze well, making last-minute assembling just that much easier. You could even garnish it with chocolate curls as well as the fresh fruit.

Torte:

2 cups	whole hazelnuts, pecans or almonds	500 mL
8	eggs, separated	8
½ cup	fruit sugar	125 mL
3 tbsp	dry fine bread crumbs	45 mL
1 tsp	baking powder	5 mL

Frosting and Filling:

2 cups	heavy cream (35%)	500 mL
¼ cup	granulated sugar	50 mL
½ tsp	vanilla or maple extract	2 mL
	Ripe fruit	

Preheat oven to 300°F (150°C).

Torte: Spread nuts on baking sheet and roast, stirring frequently, for 15 to 20 minutes or until beginning to turn dark brown. (If using hazelnuts, transfer to terry cloth tea towel and rub off skins.) Let cool. In food processor or blender, finely grind enough nuts to yield 1½ cups (375 mL). Reserve remaining toasted nuts for garnish.

Lightly grease three 9-inch (1.5 L) round cake pans and line with parchment or waxed paper. Set aside.

In very large mixing bowl, beat egg whites until stiff peaks form. In separate bowl, beat together egg yolks and sugar until thick and lemon in color; fold into egg whites until thoroughly combined. Combine bread crumbs, baking powder and ground nuts; fold very gradually into batter. Divide among prepared pans, smoothing tops with spatula or knife.

Bake in preheated 300°F (150°C) oven for 45 to 50 minutes or until golden and beginning to pull away from sides of pans. Let cool completely in pans. Carefully invert and pull off paper.

Frosting and Filling: In bowl, whip cream until foamy; gradually beat in sugar and vanilla, whipping until very stiff.

Place bottom cake layer on large flat cake plate. Gently spread with some of the whipped cream. Repeat with remaining layers, smoothing cream over sides and top. Garnish with reserved toasted nuts and/or fresh fruit. Refrigerate for several hours before serving.

Makes 12 servings.

QUEEN ELIZABETH CAKE

W̶hen I was a teenager, I used to visit a family near Holstein, just north of Mount Forest, Ontario. Lorraine, the mother, made this cake whenever she knew I was coming and it still brings back fond memories of weekends in the unspoiled rural Ontario countryside.

1 cup	boiling water	250 mL
1 cup	chopped dates	250 mL
1 tsp	baking soda	5 mL
¼ cup	shortening	50 mL
1 cup	granulated sugar	250 mL
1	egg	1
1 tsp	vanilla	5 mL
1½ cups	sifted all-purpose flour	375 mL
1 tsp	baking powder	5 mL
½ tsp	salt	2 mL
½ cup	chopped walnuts or pecans	125 mL
Coconut Topping:		
¼ cup	butter, softened	50 mL
⅓ cup	packed brown sugar	75 mL
½ cup	shredded coconut	125 mL
2 tbsp	table cream (18%)	25 mL

Preheat oven to 350°F (180°C).

In small bowl, pour boiling water over dates. Stir in baking soda; let stand until cool.

In large bowl, beat together shortening, sugar, egg and vanilla until light and fluffy. Stir together flour, baking powder and salt; add to creamed mixture alternately with date mixture and combine well. Fold in nuts.

Spread evenly in well-greased 8-inch (2 L) square cake pan. Bake for 30 to 35 minutes or until cake tester comes out clean when inserted into centre. (Cake will be very brown.) Let cool for 30 minutes.

Coconut Topping: In bowl, combine butter, sugar, coconut and cream. Spread evenly over top of cooled cake. Broil 4 to 6 inches (10 to 15 cm) from heat for just a few minutes or until browned lightly. Let cool. *Makes 9 to 12 servings.*

CINNAMON CARROT CAKE
WITH CREAM CHEESE FROSTING
••

There is only one carrot cake in our family. It's so popular that Nancy, our former babysitter, used it as her wedding cake. It's really, really good! If you can't find self-rising flour, add about 1 tbsp (15 mL) baking powder and ½ tsp (5 mL) salt to 2 cups (500 mL) cake-and-pastry flour.

2 cups	granulated sugar	500 mL
2 cups	self-rising flour	500 mL
2 tsp	cinnamon	10 mL
1½ cups	vegetable oil	375 mL
4	eggs	4
3 cups	grated carrots	750 mL
	Cream Cheese Frosting (p. 183)	
½ cup	chopped pecans or walnuts (optional)	125 mL

Preheat oven to 350°F (180°C).

In large mixing bowl, combine sugar, flour and cinnamon; beat in oil until mixture is light in color, about 3 minutes.

Beat in eggs, one at a time, beating for about 30 seconds after each addition. Add carrots, mixing thoroughly.

Spread in well-greased 9- x 13-inch (3.5 L) baking dish. Bake for 60 to 65 minutes or until tester inserted in centre comes out clean. Let cool in pan before spreading with Cream Cheese Frosting. Scatter with nuts (if using). *Makes 12 to 16 servings.*

CREAM CHEESE FROSTING

4 oz	cream cheese, softened	125 g
¼ cup	butter, softened	50 mL
3 cups	icing sugar	750 mL
1 tsp	grated orange rind (optional)	5 mL
	Milk, cream or orange juice	

In mixing bowl, beat together cheese and butter; beat in sugar, orange rind (if using) and enough milk to make fluffy spreadable consistency.

Makes 2 cups (500 mL).

SOUR CREAM
CHOCOLATE CHIP CAKE
••

This recipe came to us ten years ago from a young neighbor who was trying her hand at baking for the first time. The chocolate topping will stay soft for twenty minutes or so after it's out of the oven. That's the most wonderful time to serve the cake or take it to your neighbors.

⅓ cup	butter, softened	75 mL
1 cup	granulated sugar	250 mL
2	eggs	2
1⅓ cups	all-purpose flour	325 mL
1½ tsp	baking powder	7 mL
1 tsp	baking soda	5 mL
1 tsp	cinnamon	5 mL
1 cup	sour cream OR plain yogurt	250 mL
1	package (6 oz/168 g) semi-sweet chocolate chips	1

Preheat oven to 350°F (180°C).

In mixing bowl, cream butter and all but 1 tbsp (15 mL) of the sugar until light and fluffy. Set reserved sugar aside. Beat in eggs, one at a time.

In separate bowl, stir or sift together flour, baking powder, baking soda and cinnamon; add to creamed mixture alternately with sour cream. Spread evenly in lightly oiled 9- x 13-inch (3.5 L) baking dish. Sprinkle with chocolate chips to cover top entirely. Sprinkle with reserved sugar.

Bake for 35 minutes or until deep golden. *Makes 1 cake.*

LEMON JELLY ROLL

Fill this delicious roll with Lemon Curd, strawberry jam or thickened, sweetened fruit.

3	eggs, separated	3
¾ cup	granulated sugar	175 mL
3 tbsp	water	50 mL
1 cup	all-purpose flour	250 mL
1 tbsp	baking powder	15 mL
	Icing sugar	
2 cups	Lemon Curd (recipe follows)	500 mL

Preheat oven to 400°F (200°C). Line jelly roll pan with waxed paper or parchment paper.

In large bowl, beat egg whites until soft peaks form; gradually beat in ¼ cup (50 mL) of the sugar until stiff peaks form. Set aside.

In separate bowl, beat egg yolks until light in color; gradually beat in remaining sugar. Beat for 4 to 5 minutes. Add water; beat for 1 minute.

Sift flour and baking powder over yolk mixture; gently fold in egg whites.

Spread evenly in prepared pan. Bake for 12 to 15 minutes or until golden. Immediately invert onto kitchen towel that has been dusted with icing sugar. Peel off paper and gently roll cake lengthwise in towel. Let cool. When ready to fill, unroll carefully, spread with Lemon Curd and reroll without towel. *Makes 10 to 12 servings.*

LEMON CURD

4	lemons	4
2 cups	granulated sugar	500 mL
½ cup	butter	125 mL
6	eggs	6

Grate rind of two lemons; reserve. Squeeze all lemons and place both rind and juice into top of double boiler. Whisk in sugar, butter and eggs until smooth. Cover and cook over boiling water, stirring often, until thick, about 20 minutes. Ladle into glass jar; cool and refrigerate for up to 4 weeks. *Makes 3 cups (750 mL).*

LILLIAN'S CHRISTMAS CAKE

his light, delicious cake has been the only Christmas cake that I've made for years. I like to store it in the refrigerator to make slicing easier but if you have a cold room, that will work too. It will keep for several months if covered tightly and refrigerated, and it freezes well.

1 cup	unsalted butter, softened	250 mL
1 cup	granulated sugar	250 mL
3	eggs, separated	3
1 tsp	vanilla	5 mL
2 tsp	almond extract	10 mL
2¾ cups	cake-and-pastry flour	675 mL
½ tsp	salt	2 mL
1 tsp	baking powder	5 mL
½ tsp	grated nutmeg	2 mL
½ cup	warm water	125 mL
8 oz	red and green candied cherries, slivered	250 g
1 lb	sultana or golden raisins	500 g
4 oz	shredded coconut	125 g
3	slices candied pineapple, slivered	3

Preheat oven to 275°F (140°C). Grease 9- x 5-inch (2 L) loaf pan and line with brown paper. Grease paper thoroughly; set aside.

In large bowl, cream together butter and sugar thoroughly. Beat in egg yolks, one at a time. Beat in vanilla and almond extract.

In separate bowl, beat egg whites until stiff peaks form; set aside. Sift together flour, salt, baking powder and nutmeg; add to creamed mixture alternately with warm water, stirring until no dry spots remain. Fold in candied cherries, raisins, coconut and pineapple. Fold in egg whites.

Spread evenly in prepared pan. Bake for 3 hours or until tester inserted in centre comes out clean. Let cool for 10 minutes in pan. Remove to wire cake rack and let cool completely in paper. Peel off paper. To store, wrap tightly in brandy-soaked cheesecloth, then plastic wrap. Refrigerate for at least 1 week to ripen before serving.

Makes 1 loaf.

JEAN AND NORM'S
CHRISTMAS CAKE

T his is a recipe for Christmas cake that has been in our family for many years. It has also been used as a wedding cake and slices well, especially when soaked in sherry or brandy and wrapped tightly to age for a few weeks. Make it in November to serve in mid-to-late December, perhaps with a little port and strong cheese like Bavarian Blue.

1 lb	butter, softened	500 g
5 cups	packed brown sugar	1.25 L
12	eggs	12
1 tsp	almond extract	5 mL
1 tsp	vanilla	5 mL
1 cup	sour cream	250 mL
5 cups	cake-and-pastry flour	1.25 L
1 tsp	cinnamon	5 mL
1 tsp	grated nutmeg	5 mL
1 tsp	mace	5 mL
1 tsp	baking soda	5 mL
1 lb	red and green candied cherries, halved	500 g
1 lb	pitted dates, chopped	500 g
4 lb	sultana raisins	1.8 kg
1 lb	currants	500 g
½ lb	citrus peel	250 g
½ lb	whole almonds	250 g
½ lb	candied pineapple, chopped	250 g
	Brandy, rum or sherry (optional)	

Preheat oven to 275°F (140°C). Grease five 9- x 5-inch (2 L) loaf pans or equivalent volume of pans and line with several layers of waxed paper, brown paper or parchment paper. Place pan of water on lower rack of oven.

In very large bowl, cream butter until fluffy; beat in brown sugar until light in color. Beat in eggs, one at a time. Add almond extract, vanilla and sour cream.

In separate bowl, combine flour, cinnamon, nutmeg, mace and baking soda. Add cherries, dates, raisins, currants, citrus peel, almonds and pineapple; toss to coat. Fold into creamed mixture. Divide among prepared pans.

Bake for 2 to 3 hours or until tester inserted in centre comes out clean. Let cool for 10 minutes in pans. Remove to wire cake rack and let cool completely in paper. Peel off paper. To store, wrap tightly in brandy-soaked cheesecloth, then foil or plastic wrap before refrigerating. *Makes 5 cakes.*

MOCHA FROSTING

T his is a fast and delicious way of frosting that special chocolate cake. Garnish with chocolate curls and brandied cherries if you have some.

3 cups	heavy cream (35%)	750 mL
1½ cups	icing sugar	375 mL
½ cup	sifted unsweetened cocoa powder	125 mL
2 tsp	instant coffee granules	10 mL

In large mixing bowl, combine cream, icing sugar, cocoa and coffee; cover and chill for 30 minutes. Beat until stiff. *Makes 6 cups (1.5 mL), enough to fill and frost 8- or 9-inch (1.2 to 1.5 L) layer cake.*

ORANGE BUTTER ICING

This is great on carrot cake, or thin a quarter of the icing and drizzle it over a freshly baked sweet bread like the Brandied Apricot Brioche Braid (p. 124).

⅓ cup	butter, softened	75 mL
3 cups	icing sugar	750 mL
¼ cup	milk or cream	50 mL
2 tsp	grated orange or lemon rind	10 mL

In bowl, cream together butter and sugar; beat in milk until fluffy. Stir in orange rind. *Makes enough to frost one 9- x 13-inch (3.5 L) cake.*

VARIATION:

ALMOND BUTTER ICING

Substitute ½ tsp (2 mL) almond extract for the citrus rind. Have lots of toasted, slivered almonds on hand to strew all over the bread or cake you are frosting. This icing is a perfect finish for Cardamom Scented Christmas Bread (p. 126).

PIES AND TARTS

ONTARIO FRESH FRUIT TART

E very year, the luscious fruits of summer seem sweeter and juicier — perhaps that's a sign of my own old age.

When I buy fresh fruit, I like to know the variety in order to make a repeat purchase that much easier. Harcot apricots are about the only variety of that fruit available in Ontario and usually the supply cannot be depended on. They are simply too tender a fruit. But peaches are another story. Freestone Red Haven, Envoy and Jubilee are the easiest to handle. Although Bing is the name most of us think of when we see black cherries, Hedelfingen is the most widely grown variety. Be careful when purchasing these cherries because, even when they look ripe, they are not always at their peak. It is not easy to find raspberries sold by generic name although farmers at pick-your-own operations and farm markets often will share the information. Comet is one of the best raspberry varieties, followed closely by Festival, Boyne and the sweet purple Royalty.

Few desserts are more spectacular than a fresh apricot or peach tart, liberally laced with sweet dark cherries, scattered with raspberries or blackberries and sparkling with a red currant or apple jelly glaze. Bake one and enjoy the summer's bounty.

This luscious tart is one of my standbys, combining the ease of a food processor and a microwave. It's easy to make and the unbaked crust freezes so well that it's possible to make a few shells ahead for the summer's supply of fruit.

Vary the fruits used as they come into season. When our son makes this dessert, he drizzles melted semisweet chocolate over the finished product.

Crust:

1½ cups	cake-and-pastry flour	375 mL
¼ tsp	salt	1 mL
⅓ cup	chilled butter, cubed	75 mL
1	egg yolk	1
⅓ cup	ice water	75 mL

Filling:

2 cups	milk	500 mL
½ cup	granulated sugar	125 mL

3 tbsp	cornstarch	50 mL
3	egg yolks	3
2 tbsp	butter	25 mL
1 tsp	vanilla	5 mL
Topping:		
½ cup	apple or red currant jelly	125 mL
2 to 3 cups	fresh fruit (such as peeled sliced apricots or peaches, raspberries, pitted black cherries or blueberries)	500 to 750 mL

Preheat oven to 425°F (220°C).

Crust: In food processor or in bowl, combine flour, salt and butter; process by pulsing or cut in by hand until it resembles coarse crumbs. Mix egg yolk with water; sprinkle over flour mixture and pulse or toss with fork until it holds together.

Turn out onto well-floured board; roll out and fit into 10-inch (25 cm) straight-sided tart pan. Prick all over with fork; chill for 30 minutes. Bake for 15 to 20 minutes or until golden.

Filling: Meanwhile, in large microwaveable bowl, combine milk, sugar and cornstarch; microwave, uncovered, at High for 8 to 12 minutes or until bubbling and thickened, stirring every 2 minutes.

In separate bowl, whisk egg yolks; stir in some of the hot milk mixture. Return egg yolk mixture to bowl. Microwave at High for 2 minutes. Stir in butter and vanilla. Let cool completely.

Topping: In small saucepan or in microwave, melt jelly; brush enough over bottom and sides of crust to coat evenly. Spread cooled filling over crust. Arrange fruit in concentric circles over filling. Brush with remaining glaze. Refrigerate until serving. *Makes 8 to 10 servings.*

OLD-FASHIONED RHUBARB PIE

I used to think rhubarb was an over-rated fruit but when I tasted my friend Lynne's recipe for rhubarb pie, I changed my mind. Like all old-fashioned recipes, this one was her mother's.

3 cups	diced raw rhubarb	750 mL
	Unbaked 8-inch (20 cm) pie shell	
2	eggs, slightly beaten	2
¼ cup	all-purpose flour	50 mL
1½ cups	granulated sugar	375 mL
	Ice Cream	

Preheat oven to 400°F (200°C).

Spread rhubarb evenly in unbaked pie shell. In bowl, whisk together eggs, flour and sugar; pour over rhubarb. Bake for 10 minutes. Reduce heat to 350°F (180°C) and bake until puffed and richly golden, 25 to 30 minutes. Let stand for at least 1 hour before serving with ice cream.

Makes about 6 servings.

ULTIMATE SQUASH PIE

•••••••••••••••••••••••••••••••••••••

It was a long, long time before I figured out that pumpkin and squash could be used interchangeably. Now I prefer squash, especially the flavorful butternut, although I must admit to having a psychological kinship to the variety called Sweet Mama.

I freeze a few milk bags full of puréed squash for our wintertime supply. To prepare it for freezing, you can either cook smaller amounts in your microwave or steam/bake the squash with a bit of water in a tightly covered dish in the regular oven. Thaw the frozen squash before using as a buttered vegetable, or in the following recipe.

1½ cups	puréed squash (or pumpkin)	375 mL
¾ cup	granulated sugar	175 mL
1 tsp	cinnamon	5 mL
½ tsp	ground ginger	2 mL
3	eggs	3
1½ cups	milk (homogenized preferably)	375 mL
2 tbsp	butter, melted	25 mL
	Unbaked 9-inch (23 cm) Mom's Flaky Pastry shell (p. 211)	
	Whipped cream	

Preheat oven to 400°F (200°C).

In large bowl, whisk together squash, sugar, cinnamon, ginger, eggs, milk and butter; pour into unbaked pie shell. Bake for 10 minutes. Reduce heat to 350°F (180°C); bake until centre is set, 35 to 40 minutes. Serve at room temperature with whipped cream, if desired. Store any leftovers in refrigerator. *Makes about 6 servings.*

GRANDMA OVENS'
SOUR CREAM APPLE PIE

My grandmother burnt herself out running a restaurant during the later days of the Depression and early in World War II. She cooked so much for so little reward that she really began to dislike the whole operation. But I do remember her apple pies. Every now and then, I guess for old-times sake, she whipped up this recipe. It's fast and very good.

3 or 4	large tart apples	3 or 4
	Unbaked 9-inch (23 cm) Mom's Flaky Pastry shell (p. 211)	
1 cup	granulated sugar	250 mL
3 tbsp	all-purpose flour	50 mL
⅛ tsp	salt	0.5 mL
1 cup	sour cream	250 mL
1 tsp	cinnamon	5 mL
½ tsp	grated nutmeg	2 mL
2 tbsp	granulated sugar	25 mL

Preheat oven to 425°F (220°C).

Peel and slice apples into unbaked pie shell. Stir together 1 cup (250 mL) sugar, flour, salt and sour cream until smooth; pour over apples. Sprinkle with cinnamon, nutmeg and 2 tbsp (25 mL) sugar.

Bake for 15 minutes. Reduce heat to 350°F (180°C); bake for 20 to 25 minutes or until bubbling, lightly browned and set. Let cool for about 30 minutes before serving. *Makes 6 to 8 servings.*

PRAIRIE SASKATOON BERRY PIE

This is a family recipe that has been handed down for several generations in the Edmonton area. It comes via Jim Cowie from Alberta Tourism, and his "highly respected respected executive assistant," Lisa. As Jim says, "the old 'Catch 22' of this recipe is that you have to find a quantity of Saskatoon berries. Few, if any, are sold in the farm markets that flourish around the province. You simply have to plant your own bush."

Prepare a Mom's Flaky Pastry shell, recipe substituting chilled orange juice for the liquid. Then proceed with the pie.

3½ cups	Saskatoon berries	875 mL
3 tbsp	all-purpose flour	50 mL
1 cup	granulated sugar	250 mL
⅛ tsp	salt	0.5 mL
½ tsp	lemon juice	2 mL
⅓ cup	water	75 mL
1 tbsp	butter	15 mL
	9-inch (23 cm) Mom's Flaky Pastry shell (p. 211), double crust	

Preheat oven to 425°F (220°C).

Into heavy saucepan, combine berries, flour, sugar and salt; mix in lemon juice, water and butter. Bring to boil over medium heat; simmer, stirring, until sugar is dissolved and filling thickened.

On lightly floured surface, roll out half of the pastry to fit 9-inch (23 cm) pie plate; pour in filling. Roll out remaining pastry and place over filling, pinching and crimping edges. Slash a few steam vents in top.

Bake for 15 minutes. Reduce heat to 350°F (180°C) and bake for 35 to 40 minutes or until golden and bubbling. Let cool to room temperature before slicing. *Makes 6 to 8 servings.*

PERFECT PEACH STRUESEL PIE

T his pie is an autumn classic around our house. It's wonderful
served warm with ice cream or mounds of lightly sweetened
whipped cream. The struesel topping can be used instead of pastry on
any fruit or even mincemeat pie. I prefer the later varieties of peach —
Red Haven, Envoy or Jubilee — because of their sun-soaked natural
sweetness. Others will be fine, but you really need to taste them to
make sure they are as full flavored as they might be. I have found that
many growers seem to be picking them on the green side to prevent
shipping loss, but what really suffers is that great peachy flavor.

Filling:

5 cups	sliced peeled peaches	1.25 L
⅓ cup	granulated sugar	75 mL
2 tbsp	lemon juice	25 mL
¼ cup	quick-cooking tapioca	50 mL

Topping:

½ cup	rolled oats	125 mL
½ cup	packed brown sugar	125 mL
¼ cup	all-purpose flour	50 mL
⅓ cup	chilled butter, cut into bits	75 mL
¼ cup	chopped pecans	50 mL
	Unbaked deep 9-inch (23 cm)	
	Mom's Flaky Pastry shell (p. 211)	

Preheat oven to 425°F (220°C).

Filling: In large bowl, toss together peaches, sugar, lemon juice and
tapioca. Set aside.

Topping: In separate bowl, combine oats, brown sugar and flour.
With pastry blender, cut in butter until coarse and crumbly. Stir in nuts.

Pour filling into prepared pie shell. Sprinkle with topping, patting
down a little to hold in place.

Bake for 15 minutes. Reduce heat to 350°F (180°C); bake for 30 to
35 minutes or until fruit is tender and filling bubbles up around edge.

Let cool for 1 hour before serving warm. *Makes 6 to 8 servings.*

BUTTERMILK PIE

I first encountered this delicious pie in southern Nova Scotia. Since then, it has shown up in New Brunswick and even here in the Mennonite region of south-western Ontario.

4	eggs	4
¾ cup	granulated sugar	175 mL
¼ cup	all-purpose flour	50 mL
½ tsp	salt	2 mL
2 cups	buttermilk	500 mL
⅛ tsp	grated nutmeg	0.5 mL
	Unbaked 9-inch (23 cm) Mom's Flaky Pastry shell (p. 211)	

Preheat oven to 425°F (220°C).

In bowl, whisk together eggs, sugar, flour and salt until thoroughly blended; stir in buttermilk and nutmeg. Pour into prepared crust. Bake for 10 minutes. Reduce heat to 350°F (180°C); bake for 35 to 40 minutes or until centre is set. Let cool thoroughly before serving.

Makes about 8 servings.

VARIATION:

Mark Bussieres, a talented chef from Gananoque, Ontario, makes an upscale variation of this delicate pie by using a Sweet Tart Pastry (p. 212) in a springform pan and adding the following ingredients to the filling.

⅛ tsp	ground ginger	0.5 mL
	Grated rind of 1 lemon	
1 tbsp	lemon juice	15 mL
¼ tsp	cinnamon	1 mL
1 tsp	vanilla	5 mL

He bakes and cools it as above . To serve, he makes two pools of Fresh Fruit Purée (p. 93) on the chilled serving plates. He then floats the slice of buttermilk pie on them. A herb leaf would finish the garnish.

To make a ring of tiny hearts, dot sour or thick cream along the edge of the purée (professional chefs use a squeeze bottle). Draw the tip of a sharp knife through them. *Makes 8 to 10 servings.*

COCONUT CREAM PIE
WITH BUTTERMILK PASTRY
....

The pastry that I have used here is Lillian Kaplun's recipe, buttery and rich, and one of the best. It makes two shells, one for now and one which can be wrapped and frozen for later use. If you wish, you can substitute the baked, Sweet Tart Pastry shell (p. 212).

Pastry:

2½ cups	all-purpose flour	625 mL
⅛ tsp	salt	0.5 mL
1 cup	chilled butter, cut into bits	250 mL
2	egg yolks	2
5 tbsp	buttermilk	75 mL
1 tsp	lemon juice	5 mL

Filling:

2 cups	milk	500 mL
1 cup	half-and-half cream (10%)	250 mL
½ cup	granulated sugar	125 mL
⅓ cup	all-purpose flour	75 mL
½ cup	desiccated or grated coconut	125 mL
2	egg yolks	2
1 tsp	vanilla	5 mL

Meringue:

4	egg whites, at room temperature	4
¾ tsp	cream of tartar	4 mL
½ cup	granulated sugar	125 mL
1 tsp	vanilla	5 mL
	Shredded coconut	

Preheat oven to 425°F (220°C).

Pastry: In large mixing bowl, sift or stir together flour and salt; cut in butter until in coarse crumbs. Whisk together egg yolks, buttermilk and lemon juice. With fork, stir into dry ingredients until moistened, adding a little more buttermilk if necessary to moisten. Gather into ball.

On lightly floured surface, roll out half of the pastry and line 9-inch (23 cm) pie plate. Reserve remaining pastry for another use. Prick pastry shell all over with fork. Bake for 12 minutes or until golden. Let cool slightly.

Filling: In top of double boiler over boiling water, heat milk and cream for about 20 minutes or until steaming. Stir together sugar and flour; add to milk mixture and cook, stirring constantly, for 10 to 15 minutes or until thickened. Add coconut.

In small bowl, whisk egg yolks; whisk in a little of the hot milk mixture. Return egg yolk mixture to double boiler; cook for 3 to 5 minutes or until well-thickened, rich and lemony in color. Add vanilla. Set aside and let cool slightly.

Meringue: In bowl, beat egg whites until frothy. Beat in cream of tartar until soft peaks form. Gradually beat in sugar until stiff peaks form. Beat in vanilla.

Spread filling evenly over baked crust. Mound meringue over top, sealing edges so that no filling is showing. Scatter with shredded coconut.

Bake in 425°F (220°C) oven for 4 to 5 minutes or until rich golden brown. *Makes 5 to 8 servings.*

MAPLE WALNUT PIE

This is a Canadianized version of the old classic butterscotch pie that so many of us enjoyed while growing up.

Filling:

¼ cup	cornstarch	50 mL
1 cup	milk	250 mL
1 cup	dark maple syrup	250 mL
3	eggs yolks	3
1 tbsp	butter	15 mL
1 cup	chopped walnuts	250 mL

Meringue:

3	egg whites	3
¼ tsp	cream of tartar	1 mL
⅓ cup	granulated sugar	75 mL
	Baked 9-inch (23 cm) Mom's	
	Flaky Pastry shell (p. 211)	

Preheat oven to 350°F (180°C)

Filling: In very heavy saucepan or in double boiler, whisk together cornstarch and milk until smooth; pour in maple syrup. Cook over medium-low heat or simmering water, stirring constantly, until thickened.

In separate small bowl, stir egg yolks; whisk in some of the hot milk. Return egg yolk mixture to saucepan; cook until thickened and bubbling. Stir in butter and walnuts. Set aside to let cool.

Meringue: In bowl, beat egg whites until frothy. Beat in cream of tartar until soft peaks form. Gradually beat in sugar until very stiff glossy peaks form.

Pour filling into baked crust. Spread meringue over top. Bake for 10 to 12 minutes or until meringue is tipped with gold. Let cool. To serve, cut with knife that has been dipped into hot water.

Makes 6 to 8 servings.

SOUR CHERRY PIE FILLING
••

Montmorency are the classic sour cherries used in pies. Morello is another tart variety that is sometimes sold at farm markets or on roadside stands. In the late summer, pails of lightly sweetened cherries begin appearing in our local supermarkets, pitted and ready to be frozen in 4-cup (1 L) bags. (Milk bags make excellent, heavy-duty freezer containers.)

All winter long we can whip down to the freezer to pull out enough cherries for a pie, Danish Pastry (p. 150) or for a cake filling. Frozen cherries make preparing homemade pie filling a snap.

4 cups	frozen cherries, partially or completely thawed	1 L
1¼ cups	granulated sugar	300 mL
⅓ cup	cornstarch	75 mL
2 tbsp	butter (optional)	25 mL

In heavy saucepan over medium-high heat, cover and bring cherries to boil quickly, stirring several times. Combine sugar and cornstarch; add to boiling cherries all at once. Cook for 2 to 3 minutes or until thickened and bubbling. (If you cook it any longer the cherries will loose their brillance.) Add butter. Let cool.

Makes 4 cups (1 L), enough for 9-inch (23 cm) deep-dish pie.

CARLETON COUNTRY
VENISON MINCEMEAT

Seasons such as Christmas often sound nostalgic chords, especially when we are far away from our childhood home.

I met Jill Killeen in one of Vancouver's poshest hotels, where she is involved with public relations. As we chatted about food, she revealed her rural New Brunswick heritage and how she's missed the closeness of her family and their well-rooted sense of community. One of her favorite seasons there is Christmas, when her father has bagged his yearly deer and her mother has made this pungent mincemeat from the lean cuts.

As a treat for the stirrers, I think that you should let them pour some of the hot mincemeat over French vanilla ice cream.

4 lb	lean venison roast, from neck portion	2 kg
1 lb	suet	500 g
10 lb	sour apples (like Courtland), peeled, cored and coarsely chopped	4.5 kg
6 lb	seedless raisins	3 kg
	Juice and rind of 2 oranges	
	Juice and rind of 3 lemons	
2 cups	packed brown sugar	500 mL
2 cups	granulated sugar	500 mL
1 cup	molasses	250 mL
1 cup	apple cider vinegar	250 mL
½ to 1 cup	homemade jam	125 to 250 mL
1 tbsp	salt	15 mL
2	whole nutmegs, grated	2
3 tbsp	ground cinnamon	50 mL
1 tbsp	ground cloves	15 mL
1 to 2 cups	Apple juice or cider	250 to 500 mL

Preheat oven to 350°F (160°C).

In covered roasting pan, cook meat with ½ cup (125 mL) water for 3½ to 4 hours or until well done. Remove from pan and let cool for 30 minutes. Grind in meat grinder along with suet.

Meanwhile, in large heavy pot, cook apples with 2 cups (500 mL) water until soft, about 25 minutes, stirring frequently and adding water as needed to prevent sticking. Add meat, raisins, orange rind and juice, lemon rind and juice, brown sugar, granulated sugar, molasses, cider vinegar, jam, salt, nutmeg, cinnamon and cloves. Moisten with apple juice if necessary. Bring to gentle boil over medium heat; reduce heat and simmer, covered, for 3 to 4 hours or until thickened and brown, adding apple juice as needed to prevent drying out. To store, ladle into clean jars and freeze or refrigerate for up to 1 month.

Makes 24 to 28 cups (6 to 7 L).

For me, making meringue was one of the most difficult things to master in my kitchen. After my last failure (the pie was great but the topping was miserable), I decided to shelve my pride and call on the Ontario Egg Marketing Board. They gave me the lowdown. Now I am able to pile my pies high and make lightly golden crisp creations to be filled with fruit and cream.

Use only a metal or glass bowl.

Separate eggs when they are cold. Be sure that no yolk slips in with the white.

Then let the egg whites stand for 30 minutes to reach room temperature. They will whip to a greater volume than when cold.

The secret of a successful meringue is producing a stable egg white foam. The egg whites begin as a liquid that incorporates air during beating, forming first in large bubbles (the frothy stage), then in countless tiny air cells. The liquid has become a white foam, smooth and moist in appearance.

Unless stabilized, the foam will return to the liquid state. This is why acid ingredients such as cream of tartar, vinegar or lemon juice are added at the frothy stage.

Sugar also stabilizes the foam but, at the same time, it retards or slows down the foam formation. For this reason, I recommend that the sugar be added slowly, a tablespoon at a time, once the foam has reached the soft peak stage.

"Soft peaks" are mounds of egg white that, as you lift the beaters, fold over onto themselves.

"Stiff peaks" are mounds whose peaks remain upright after you lift the beaters away.

SOFT MERINGUE TOPPING FOR PIES

3	egg whites, at room temperature	3
½ tsp	cream of tartar	2 mL
⅓ cup	granulated sugar	75 mL
½ tsp	vanilla	2 mL

In bowl, beat egg whites until frothy. Beat in cream of tartar until soft peaks form. Gradually add sugar, a tablespoonful (15 mL) at a time, beating constantly until sugar is dissolved and stiff, glossy peaks form when beaters are lifted. Beat in vanilla.

Pile lightly on hot pie filling, making sure to seal meringue to crust so it will not shrink while baking. Bake in 350°F (180°C) oven for 8 to 10 minutes, 425°F (220°C) for 4 minutes, or until set and delicately browned. Let cool at room temperature.

Makes enough for one 9-inch (23 cm) pie.

HARD MERINGUE SHELLS

These shells may be made days ahead of serving if stored in an airtight container. Fill them with ice cream or custard and fruit. For a superb garnish, drizzle them with a little melted bittersweet or semisweet chocolate.

4	egg whites	4
½ tsp	cream of tartar	2 mL
1 cup	granulated sugar	250 mL
1 tsp	vanilla	5 mL

In large bowl, beat egg whites until frothy. Beat in cream of tartar until soft peaks form. Gradually add sugar, a tablespoonful (15 mL) at a time, beating constantly until sugar is dissolved and stiff glossy peaks form when beaters are lifted. Beat in vanilla.

With spoon, shape about ⅓ cup (75 mL) of the meringue at a time into "nests" on parchment-lined baking sheet paper, or ungreased paper. Make them about 3 inches (8 cm) wide, building up edge to form rim.

Bake in preheated 250°F (120°C) oven for 1 hour or until firm. Turn off oven and let meringues cool in oven (with door closed) for 1 more hour.

Remove from baking sheets and store in airtight container.

Makes 12 shells.

PEGGY MORRIS'
AMAZING BUTTER TARTS

B utter tarts are much like pastry: you have to have a certain touch. Unfortunately, I've only tasted the "best recipe." Mine, no matter how hard I try, never have quite the same gooey texture. This, however, turned out to be my first real success. . . an honest-to-goodness winner.

1 cup	raisins	250 mL
2	eggs	2
⅓ cup	corn syrup	75 mL
1 cup	packed brown sugar	250 mL
3 tbsp	butter, melted	50 mL
½ cup	chopped nuts	125 mL
18	Sweet Tart Pastry shells (p. 212).	18

In small bowl, cover raisins with boiling water; let soak for 20 to 30 minutes. Drain and set aside.

Preheat oven to 450°F (230°F).

In mixing bowl, whisk eggs thoroughly. Beat in corn syrup, sugar, butter, nuts and raisins. Pour evenly into tart shells. Bake on middle rack for 5 minutes. Reduce heat to 350°F (180°C); open oven door for 15 to 20 seconds to bring temperature down rapidly. Bake for 15 minutes longer or until bubbling and deep golden brown. Let cool for 10 to 15 minutes before removing from pan. *Makes 18 tarts.*

RASPBERRY COCONUT TARTS

This recipe comes from an old handwritten cookbook from one of Elora, Ontario's original families. Small blobs of ink and cooking stains dot the yellowed, fragile pages. I feel privileged to be able to glimpse these records of turn-of-the-century family life.

Plop a bit of rich jam into the bottom of your tart shells. Raspberry is great, but so is strawberry. Cherry jam is exquisite.

2 cups	flaked sweetened coconut	500 mL
¼ cup	butter, melted	50 mL
2	eggs, beaten	2
½ cup	packed brown sugar	125 mL
	Jam	
12	unbaked Sweet Tart Pastry shells (p. 212)	12

Preheat oven to 425°F (220°C).

In bowl, stir together coconut, butter, eggs and sugar until thoroughly combined. Drop small spoonful of jam into each tart shell. Cover completely with coconut mixture. Bake for 5 minutes. Reduce heat to 350°F (180°C); bake for 12 to 15 minutes or until puffed and golden. *Makes 12 large tarts.*

BUTTERY WHOLE WHEAT PASTRY

I love this recipe because it's so incredibly fast and very tasty. Add the salt only if you're using unsalted butter.

2 cups	stone-ground whole wheat flour	500 mL
2 tbsp	packed brown sugar	25 mL
¼ tsp	salt (optional)	1 mL
¾ cup	chilled butter, cut into small bits	175 mL
⅓ cup	ice water	75 mL

In food processor, combine flour, sugar, and salt (if using); process for 2 to 3 seconds just to combine.

With machine running, add butter. Immediately pour in ice water; process until it begins to form lumps. Wrap soft dough in plastic wrap; refrigerate for 20 to 30 minutes before rolling out on well-floured surface. *Makes enough for 1 double-crust 8-inch (20 cm) pie or 1 single-crust 9-inch (23 cm) pie shell and 8 to 10 tarts.*

MOM'S FLAKY PASTRY

I like to make a number of pie shells ahead of time and freeze them in plastic grocery bags, ready to pull out and use for quiches or pies. When baking the shells, it's important, according to Mom, to bake them at a high temperature (425°F/220°C) for 10 to 12 minutes before filling. This amount makes about 4 to 5 pie shells.

5 cups	cake-and-pastry flour	1.25 mL
½ tsp	salt	2 mL
2 cups	chilled shortening	500 mL
1¼ cups	ice water	300 mL

In large bowl, blend flour and salt. With pastry blender, cut in cold shortening until in fine crumbs. With fork, stir in ice water, ¼ cup (50 mL) at a time, until dough holds together when pinched. Gather pastry into ball. Cut off about one-quarter and roll out on well-floured surfaced until about ¼ inch (5 m) thickness.

Fit into pie plate; trim and flute edges. Freeze and store in airtight container for up to 4 weeks. Place layers of waxed paper between shells if storing them in pie plates.

Makes four 9-inch (23 cm) single crust pie shells and 12 tarts.

SWEET TART PASTRY

·····································

T his is a sweeter pastry to be used for desserts such as Buttermilk Pie (p. 199) or Grandma Ovens' Sour Cream Apple Pie (p. 196).

2 ½ cups	cake-and-pastry flour	625 mL
¼ cup	granulated sugar	50 mL
½ tsp	salt	2 mL
1 cup	chilled unsalted butter, cut into bits	250 mL
¾ cup	ice water	175 mL

In bowl, stir together flour, sugar and salt. With pastry blender, cut in butter until in fine crumbs. With fork, stir in ice water, ¼ cup (50 mL) at a time, until dough can be gathered up into ball.

Turn dough out onto lightly floured surface. Flour rolling pin and upper surface of dough. Roll out half of the pastry at a time to form 10- to 12-inch (25 to 30 cm) circle. Lay gently in pie plate. Trim and flute edges; add trimming to remaining dough. Repeat. Cover shells with plastic wrap if not using immediately; chill or freeze.

Makes two 9-inch (23 cm) pie shells or 24 large tart shells.

HOMESTYLE DESSERTS, ICE CREAM AND CANDY

MY MOTHER'S APPLE CRISP

I was going to name this recipe "The Quintessential" or "The Best" or "The Ultimate," but on reflection, when I call it "My Mother's" the title says it all. Love and good food certainly are twins. Serve warm with milk, cream or ice cream.

5 cups	sliced peeled apples (Idared, Northern Spy or other firm tart apple)	1.25 L
1 tbsp	lemon juice	15 mL
⅓ cup	unbleached all-purpose flour	75 mL
1 cup	rolled oats	250 mL
½ cup	coarsely chopped nuts	125 mL
1 cup	packed brown sugar	250 mL
½ tsp	salt (optional)	2 mL
½ tsp	cinnamon	2 mL
⅓ cup	butter or margarine, melted	75 mL

Preheat oven to 350°F (180°C).

Spread apples evenly in buttered 9-inch (2.5 L) square baking dish; sprinkle with lemon juice. Set aside.

In mixing bowl, stir together flour, rolled oats, nuts, brown sugar, salt (if using) and cinnamon. With fork, blend in melted butter. Sprinkle over apples. Bake for 30 minutes or until tender and golden.

Makes 6 to 8 servings.

RHUBARB BROWN BETTY

If you have a choice of rhubarb, either to purchase or to plant, try to find the kind named "strawberry." Its stems are a delicate pink and the stalks seem less stringy than other varieties. Serve this dessert warm with table cream.

4 cups	diced fresh rhubarb	1 L
1 cup	granulated sugar	250 mL
1 cup	rolled oats	250 mL
3 tbsp	all-purpose flour	50 mL
⅛ tsp	salt	0.5 mL
¾ cup	packed brown sugar	175 mL
½ tsp	cinnamon	2 mL
⅓ cup	butter, softened	75 mL

Preheat oven to 350°F (180°C).

Toss rhubarb with granulated sugar; spread evenly in buttered 8-inch (2 L) square baking dish. Set aside.

In mixing bowl, combine rolled oats, flour, salt, brown sugar and cinnamon. With pastry blender or hands, cut or rub in butter until in crumbs. Sprinkle over rhubarb. Bake for 35 to 40 minutes or until browned and bubbling around edges. *Makes 6 to 8 servings.*

POUDING CHÔMEUR
(LAZY COOK'S PUDDING)

T his is one of those recipes that look odd but tastes really, really good. The recipe comes from the Laurentians in Quebec — a perfect après-ski dessert. When the pudding is baked, the sauce will be on the bottom.

Pudding:

1 cup	granulated sugar	250 mL
2 cups	unbleached all-purpose flour	500 mL
2 tsp	baking powder	10 mL
⅛ tsp	salt	0.5 mL
1 cup	milk	250 mL
¼ cup	butter, melted	50 mL

Sauce:

¾ cup	granulated sugar	175 mL
¾ cup	packed brown sugar	175 mL
1 cup	water	250 mL
¼ cup	butter, melted	50 mL
1 tsp	vanilla or maple extract	5 mL

Preheat oven to 350°F (180°).

Pudding: In bowl, stir together sugar, flour, baking powder and salt; whisk in milk and melted butter to make fairly stiff batter. Turn into buttered 8-cup (2 L) glass casserole. Set aside.

Sauce: In heavy saucepan, combine granulated and brown sugars and water; bring to boil to dissolve sugar. Remove from heat; stir in butter and vanilla. Pour immediately over pudding base. Bake for 35 to 45 minutes or until puffy, bubbling and golden brown. *Makes 6 servings.*

CHOCOLATE PUDDING

Have you ever read the ingredient list on the side of a chocolate pudding box? To me, it's downright scary. And making a real pudding is so incredibly easy!

If you want a chocolate pie, simply pour the partially cooled pudding into a fully baked 8-inch (20 cm) pie shell, chill and dollop with whipped cream. Serve the pudding as is or with whipped or ice cream.

3 cups	milk (whole or partially skimmed)	750 mL
¾ cup	granulated sugar	175 mL
3 tbsp	unsweetened cocoa powder	50 mL
3 tbsp	cornstarch	50 mL
2	eggs	2
1 tsp	vanilla	5 mL
2 tbsp	butter	25 mL

In heavy saucepan, warm milk over medium heat until steaming and almost boiling. Meanwhile, stir or sift together sugar, cocoa and cornstarch until no tiny lumps remain. Add to saucepan and cook, stirring constantly, until bubbling and thickened.

In bowl, whisk eggs well; stir in a little of the hot milk mixture. Return egg mixture to saucepan and cook, stirring constantly, over medium-low heat until just beginning to bubble again. Remove from heat. Stir in vanilla and butter. Pour into serving dish; let cool for 15 to 30 minutes before covering and refrigerating. *Makes 4 to 6 servings.*

DUTCH APPLE PUDDING

Nancy Wideman's cool, dry basement is a storehouse of wonderful autumn produce: a huge bin of potatoes, spaghetti squash, acorn squash, canned tomatoes, tomato juice, drying onions and summer sausage hanging from the rafters, grape juice with the fruit still floating, chili sauce, vegetable soup, canned green beans, yellow beans in glass jars, sauerkraut, peaches in syrup, crocks of pickles, vegetable soup, and apples. . . bushels of apples, Greenings, Spys, Delicious, McIntosh, Blenheim orange. Upstairs in a warm, dry closet are bags of dried apples or "schnitz."

This fast dessert is great for using up apples that aren't just as perfect as they might be. Nancy uses the last of her apple harvest this way or she'll make it into apple schnitz or sauce. Serve with cream or ice cream.

¼ cup	shortening	50 mL
¾ cup	granulated sugar	175 mL
1	egg	1
1½ cups	all-purpose flour	375 mL
2½ tsp	baking powder	12 mL
½ tsp	salt	2 mL
½ cup	milk	125 mL
3 or 4	medium-sized apples, peeled, cored and cut into wedges	3 or 4
2 tbsp	packed brown sugar	25 mL
1 tsp	cinnamon	5 mL

Preheat oven to 375°F (190°C). Grease or butter 9-inch (2.5 L) square cake pan.

In mixing bowl, cream together shortening and sugar; beat in egg. Stir or sift together flour, baking powder and salt. Add to creamed mixture alternately with milk, stirring until no dry spots remain. Spread in prepared pan; insert apple wedges all over top.

Mix brown sugar with cinnamon; sprinkle over batter. Bake for 45 to 50 minutes or until puffed, beginning to brown and cake tester inserted in centre comes out clean. *Makes 6 servings.*

GRANDPA'S
FAVORITE BREAD PUDDING

R emember that this is one of those approximate-quantity recipes.
Once you've mastered it — and that should take about one try,
you can vary it by adding different kinds of bread, dried fruit or even
chunks of fresh fruit. One of my favorite variations has a dash of dark
rum and some sliced, overripe bananas. Serve this warm with lightly
sweetened whipped cream, table cream or just milk.

5 or 6	slices stale white bread	5 or 6
	Butter	
2	eggs, beaten	2
2 cups	milk	500 mL
½ tsp	vanilla	2 mL
½ tsp	almond extract	2 mL
½ cup	packed brown sugar	125 mL
½ tsp	cinnamon	2 mL
½ tsp	grated nutmeg	2 mL
½ cup	sultana raisins or currants	125 mL

Preheat oven to 325°F (160°C).

Trim crust from bread if heavy and thick. Butter bread lightly; tear
into 1- or 2-inch (2.5 or 5 cm) chunks. Set aside. In bowl, whisk
together eggs, milk, vanilla and almond extract; set aside. Combine
brown sugar, cinnamon and nutmeg.

In buttered 8-cup (2 L) casserole, layer bread, sugar mixture and
raisins; pour milk mixture over top to almost cover bread. Place casserole in larger pan in 1 inch (2.5 cm) of very hot water. Bake, uncovered, for 1 hour or until top is golden and custard is set. Serve warm.

Makes 4 to 6 servings.

RICE AND RAISIN PUDDING

Using cooked rice, this pudding is exceptionally easy. I often steam extra rice at dinnertime just so I can make this dessert. It's good either warm or cold, served as is, or with cream.

½ cup	granulated sugar	125 mL
2 tbsp	cornstarch	25 mL
2 cups	milk	500 mL
½ cup	sultana raisins	125 mL
2	eggs, beaten	2
2 tbsp	butter	25 mL
1 tsp	vanilla	5 mL
2 cups	cooked long-grain rice	500 mL

In top of double boiler over boiling water, stir together sugar, cornstarch, milk and raisins; cook, stirring occasionally, until thickened and steaming, 20 to 25 minutes.

Whisk a little of the hot mixture into beaten eggs; return egg mixture to saucepan. Cook for 2 to 3 minutes. Stir in butter, vanilla and rice. Transfer to glass serving bowl; let cool slightly before serving.

Makes 4 to 6 servings.

RISKREM
· · · · · · · · · · · · · · · ·

Peggy Austin-Johanssen says that although this dessert is "popular throughout the year, it is the typical Norwegian Christmas dessert. At that time, one whole almond is placed in it and the finder gets a special gift." This dessert is even more Christmas-like when topped with raspberry Fresh Fruit Purée (p. 93).

¾ cup	uncooked rice	175 mL
4 cups	milk	1 L
1 tsp	salt	5 mL
½ cup	granulated sugar	125 mL
½ tsp	almond extract	2 mL
½ cup	slivered almonds	125 mL
1	whole almond	1
2 cups	heavy cream	500 mL
	Granulated sugar	

In top of double boiler over boiling water, combine rice, milk and salt; cook, stirring often, until rice is tender and milk is absorbed, about 1½ hours. Stir in sugar and almond extract. Transfer to glass bowl; cover and chill for 1 to 2 hours.

Just before serving, stir in slivered almonds and whole almond. Whip cream, sweetening with sugar to taste; fold into rice mixture.

Makes 8 to 10 servings.

VARIATION:

Fold 2 cups (500 mL) drained crushed pineapple into completed dessert. Chill and serve as above.

HOT LEMON SOUFFLÉ PUDDING

Linda Myres shares this recipe from her Vancouver home. She says her guests frequently comment that this tangy pudding is "just like Grandmother used to make." As well as blueberries, you can perhaps garnish it with a leaf or two of a citrusy plant like lemon geranium or lemon balm.

¼ cup	butter, softened	50 mL
½ tsp	salt	2 mL
2 cups	granulated sugar	500 mL
¼ cup	all-purpose flour	50 mL
	Juice and rind of 2 lemons	
6	eggs, separated	6
2 cups	milk, scalded	500 mL
	Blueberries	

Preheat oven to 350°F (180°C).

In bowl, cream together butter, salt and sugar until light; beat in flour, lemon juice and rind until smooth. Lightly beat egg yolks; blend into creamed mixture. Whisk in scalded milk.

In bowl, beat eggs whites until stiff peaks form; fold into batter. Pour into buttered 8-cup (2 L) soufflé dish or casserole. Place dish in larger pan that has 1 inch (2.5 cm) very hot water. Bake for 45 to 60 minutes or until browned, firm and sauce begins to thicken. To serve, garnish with blueberries. *Makes 6 servings.*

CREAMY BAKED CUSTARD

• •

Few desserts are so basic or so good. Double this recipe and use as the filling for a plain 9-inch (23 cm) custard pie. My mother used to scatter finely chopped dates all over the unbaked pie crust, fill it with custard and sprinkle it with a little cinnamon and nutmeg before she popped it into the oven . . . it was my favorite pie!

1½ cups	milk	375 mL
3 tbsp	granulated sugar	50 mL
½ tsp	vanilla	2 mL
2	eggs, well beaten	2
	Cinnamon	

Preheat oven to 350°F (180°C).

In bowl, whisk or blend together milk, sugar and vanilla until sugar is dissolved. Beat in eggs until foamy and completely blended.

Pour into 4 lightly buttered custard cups; place in pan that has about 1-inch (2.5 cm) hot water. Dust tops with cinnamon. Bake on centre rack for about 1 hour and 20 minutes or until set and knife inserted into centre comes out clean and edges and tops are golden. *Makes 4 servings.*

****

To Bake A Custard Pie

Fill an unbaked pie shell with unbaked custard and bake, without the water bath, beginning at 425°F (220°C) for 10 minutes and then reducing the heat to 350°F (180°C) to finish baking. A knife will come out clean when inserted into the centre of the pie.

****

APPLE CUSTARD TORTE

···

T his is Joanne Yolles' variation of Lillian Kaplun's dessert. If you
dine at Scaramouche in Toronto, you may recognize it. Dust
with sifted icing sugar if desired.

Base:		
½ cup	butter, softened	125 mL
¾ cup	granulated sugar	175 mL
2	eggs	2
1⅓ cups	all-purpose flour	325 mL
2 tsp	baking powder	10 mL
8 to 10	Northern Spy apples, peeled and cut into eighths	8 to 10
½ tsp	cinnamon	2 mL
Custard:		
2 tbsp	whipping cream (35%)	25 mL
½ cup	granulated sugar	125 mL
2	eggs	2

Preheat oven to 350°F (180°C). Grease 10-inch (3 L) springform pan
generously; line with circle of parchment paper or waxed paper.

Base: In large bowl, cream together butter, sugar and eggs until
fluffy. Sift together flour and baking powder; carefully fold into
creamed mixture until no dry spots remain. Spread evenly in prepared
pan. Stand apples on end in batter until entire surface is covered.
Sprinkle with cinnamon. Bake for 60 to 75 minutes or until apples are
tender.

Custard: Whisk together cream, sugar and eggs; pour over baked
base. Bake in 325°F (160°C) oven for 20 to 30 minutes or until custard
is set. Let cool for 10 to 15 minutes before loosening from pan and
sliding onto plate. Serve warm. *Makes 10 to 12 servings.*

LILLIAN PHILLIPS'
CHRISTMAS PLUM PUDDING
••

Over the past 65 years, Lillian has been making this pudding for her family and friends. In our house, it is as traditional as the Christmas tree.

Make it in October or early November to allow it time to ripen. And don't skimp on the brandy! When reheating, "The longer you steam it the darker and the better it will be," says Lillian. To serve, pour some brandy (⅓ cup (75 mL) will do) over it. Light the brandy and bring to the table. Serve with Brandy Sauce.

1 cup	all-purpose flour	250 mL
1 tsp	baking soda	5 mL
1 tsp	salt	5 mL
1 tsp	cinnamon	5 mL
¾ tsp	mace	4 mL
¼ tsp	allspice	1 mL
¼ tsp	grated nutmeg	1 mL
1½ cups	sultana raisins	375 mL
2 cups	currants	500 mL
1 cup	mixed candied peel	250 mL
½ cup	candied lemon peel	125 mL
½ cup	whole glazed cherries	125 mL
1½ cups	soft finely ground bread crumbs	375 mL
2 cups	ground suet	500 mL
1 cup	packed brown sugar	250 mL
3	eggs, beaten	3
¼ cup	orange juice	50 mL
⅓ cup	molasses	75 mL
⅔ cup	brandy	150 mL
	Brandy Sauce (p. 227)	

Into large bowl, sift together flour, baking soda, salt, cinnamon, mace, allspice and nutmeg. Stir in raisins, currants, mixed peel, lemon peel and cherries to coat thoroughly. Add bread crumbs, suet and brown sugar; stir again.

In bowl, whisk together eggs, orange juice, molasses and brandy; add all at once to dry ingredients, stirring until completely combined.

Divide batter among three 4-cup (1 L) greased pudding bowls, smoothing surfaces. Completely cover surfaces with rounds of buttered waxed paper. Place each bowl in centre of old tea towel. With strong string, tie towel under rim of each bowl, leaving four "tails." Tie opposite tails together tightly to make sling with which to handle bowls.

Place bowls into Dutch ovens or large cooking pots. Pour in enough water to come about one-third up side of bowls. Cover tightly and bring to boil over medium heat. Reduce heat and let puddings steam for 4 hours, replenishing water when necessary. Remove from pot and let cool in bowl. Refrigerate, well wrapped, until Christmastime.

To serve, resteam pudding for 1 to 2 hours. Unwrap, loosen edges and invert onto large serving dish. Serve with Brandy Sauce.

Makes 16 servings.

BRANDY SAUCE

Spoon this boozy sauce over Christmas plum pudding or simply over ice cream or cake. Custard powder is found in the pudding section of most supermarkets. This sauce may be made ahead of time and re-heated in a double boiler. It will have to be stirred until smooth.

1¼ cups	packed brown sugar	300 mL
¼ cup	custard powder	50 mL
2 cups	water	500 mL
¼ cup	butter	50 mL
1 tsp	brandy flavoring	5 mL
½ cup	brandy	125 mL

In heavy saucepan, combine brown sugar and custard powder; whisk in water and cook over medium-low heat, stirring constantly, until thickened, 7 to 10 minutes. Stir in butter until melted. Stir in brandy flavoring and brandy. Serve warm. Refrigerate any leftover sauce. *Makes 3 cups (750 mL).*

NANCY WIDEMAN'S EASTER CHEESE

This custardy cheese is sliced into wedges and served with the season's fresh maple syrup poured generously over each portion. Although the Wideman's use their own unpasteurized milk, I substitute homogenized milk from the grocery.

8 cups	whole milk	2 L
5	eggs	5
1½ cups	buttermilk	375 mL
1 tsp	white vinegar	5 mL
½ tsp	salt	2 mL

In heavy saucepan, heat milk until simmering. In bowl, beat together eggs, buttermilk, vinegar and salt. Gradually pour into steaming milk; cook over medium-low heat, stirring constantly to prevent scorching, for 15 to 20 minutes or until mixture separates and produces distinct curds.

Transfer to cheesecloth-lined colander; let drip, squeezing periodically, for about 1 hour. Serve immediately or wrap and refrigerate for up to 1 week. *Makes about 10 servings.*

CANADIAN VANILLA ICE CREAM

For a Christmas treat, add ⅓ cup (75 mL) diced candied peel and ½ cup (125 mL) drained, chopped maraschino cherries to this ice cream before freezing the custard. In the summer, fold in 2 cups (500 mL) fresh seasonal berries—raspberries, small wild strawberries, and blueberries are great. In the autumn, chop a sweet juicy peach or a handful of peeled ripe apricots into the ice cream. This list can be as long as your imagination.

1 cup	table cream (18%)	250 mL
3 cups	whole milk	750 mL
⅔ cup	granulated sugar	150 mL
8	egg yolks	8
½ cup	maple syrup	125 mL
1 tsp	vanilla	5 mL

In very heavy saucepan, heat cream, milk and sugar until beginning to steam. Meanwhile, in bowl, beat egg yolks until light in color; whisk in some of the hot milk. Return egg yolk mixture to saucepan; cook over medium heat, stirring constantly, until thick enough to coat back of spoon, about 10 minutes. Stir in maple syrup and vanilla. Remove from heat and let cool completely before freezing in ice cream machine according to manufacturer's directions. *Makes about 6 cups (1.5 L).*

RASPBERRY FROMASJ

• •

According to Peggy Austin-Johanssen, Norwegians love raspberries. This easy, light ice cream is their variation of frozen raspberry mousse.

1	package (425 g) frozen raspberries in light syrup OR	1
1¾ cups	lightly sweetened crushed raspberries	425 mL
1 tbsp	unflavored gelatin	15 mL
¼ cup	cold water	50 mL
3	eggs, separated	3
¾ cup	granulated sugar Juice and rind of 1 lemon	175 mL
1 cup	heavy cream (35%) Whole raspberries and slivered almonds	250 mL

In top of double boiler, heat raspberries until steaming. Meanwhile, sprinkle gelatin over cold water; let stand for 5 minutes to soften. Add to raspberries, stirring to dissolve.

Whisk together egg yolks and ¼ cup (50 mL) of the sugar; stir into raspberry mixture and cook, stirring often, until slightly thickened. Add lemon juice and rind. Transfer to glass bowl; cover and chill until beginning to thicken. Beat until frothy.

In separate bowl, beat egg whites until soft peaks form; gradually beat in remaining sugar until stiff peaks form. Fold into raspberry mixture. Whip cream until stiff; fold into raspberry mixture.

Spoon into individual glass dishes or lightly oiled mould. Freeze until firm.

If using mould, loosen edges with very sharp knife and dip quickly into hot water; invert onto serving plate. Rap plate on counter if dessert is stubborn. Garnish with whole raspberries and slivered almonds. *Makes 4 to 6 servings.*

MOM'S FAMOUS FUDGE

Add 3 coarsely diced squares of semisweet chocolate to the final mixture to make a creamy chocolate variation. Just to show my age, I have also made this particular variation using half of a ten cent bar of milk chocolate.

3 cups	packed light brown sugar	750 mL
⅓ cup	golden corn syrup	75 mL
⅓ cup	whole milk	75 mL
3 tbsp	butter	50 mL
1 tsp	vanilla	5 mL
½ cup	chopped walnuts or pecans (optional)	125 mL

Butter 9-inch (2.5 L) square pan.

In heavy saucepan, combine sugar, corn syrup, milk and butter; bring to boil over medium heat, stirring constantly to dissolve sugar. Insert candy thermometer so that it does not touch bottom of pan. Cook, without stirring, until temperature reaches 238°F (115°C) or soft ball stage, watching carefully during final minutes of cooking.

Remove from heat; stir in vanilla, and nuts (if using). With wooden spoon, beat until fudge begins to thicken, 7 to 10 minutes. Pour into prepared pan. Let cool, scoring with sharp knife before fully set.

Makes 2 to 3 dozen pieces.

PEANUT BRITTLE

I wonder how many people have enjoyed the pleasures of home-made nut brittle? Use Canadian peanuts if you can get them. The little red-skinned nuts are perfect in this candy. Reduce or omit salt if the peanuts are salted.

2 cups	peanuts (with skins on)	500 mL
1½ cups	corn syrup	375 mL
¾ cup	granulated sugar	175 mL
6 tbsp	peanut butter	90 mL
¾ tsp	baking soda	4 mL
1 tsp	salt	5 mL

Generously butter baking sheet; spread peanuts evenly over top. Set aside.

In heavy saucepan, stir together corn syrup and sugar; bring to boil over medium heat, stirring constantly. Insert candy thermometer so that it does not touch bottom of pan. Cook, without stirring, until temperature reaches 290°F (143°C) or light crack stage. Remove from heat.

Meanwhile, combine peanut butter, baking soda and salt. As soon as pan is removed from heat, quickly stir in peanut butter mixture to make creamy foam. Pour evenly over peanuts; let harden before breaking into chunks. Store in airtight container. *Makes 2 lb (1 kg)*.

INDEX

· · · · · · · · · · ·

ABOUT THE AUTHOR

•••••••••••••••••••••••••••••••••••••••

Anita Stewart is the author of such bestselling cookbooks as *The Farmer's Market Cookbook*, *The St. Lawrence Market Cookbook*, and *Anita Stewart's Country Inn Cookbook*. She has written for numerous newspapers and magazines including *Canadian Living*, *Harrowsmith*, and *City and Country Home*. Stewart is a member of both the International Association of Cooking Professionals and the Society of American Travel Writers. She lives with her family in Elora, Ontario.

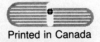
Printed in Canada